To my dear Friend,
Jean Barrett,
with my very best wishes
and sincere admiration for
her meritorious work in
myriad fields

Mel B. Yoken
7 May 1987
New Bedford

THE LETTERS
(1971-1977)
OF
ROBERT MOLLOY

THE LETTERS
(1971-1977)
OF
ROBERT MOLLOY

Edited by

Melvin B. Yoken

Studies in American Literature
Volume 1

The Edwin Mellen Press
Lewiston•Queenston
Lampeter

Library of Congress Cataloging-in-Publication Data

Molloy, Robert, 1906-1977.
  [Correspondence. Selections]
  The letters (1971-1977) of Robert Molloy / edited by Melvin B.
Yoken.
    p. cm. -- (Studies in American literature ; v. 1)
  Includes index.
  ISBN 0-88946-167-8
  1. Molloy, Robert, 1906-1977--Correspondence. 2. Novelists,
American--20th century--Correspondence. I. Yoken, Melvin B.
II. Title. III. Series: Studies in American literature (Lewiston,
  N.Y.) ; v. 1.
  PS3525.0219Z48 1989
  813'.54--dc19
  [B]   88-12711
                                                            CIP

This is volume 1 in the continuing series
Studies in American Literature
Volume 1 ISBN 0-88946-167-8
SAL Series ISBN 0-88946-166-X

The Edwin Mellen Press

Box 450   Box 67
Lewiston, New York   Queenston, Ontario
14092 USA   CANADA L0S 1L0
                        Mellen House
                   Lampeter, Dyfed, Wales
                  UNITED KINGDOM SA48 7DY

            Printed in the United States of America

TO MY CHERISHED FRIEND,
MARION MOLLOY

AND IN MEMORY OF ANOTHER
CHERISHED FRIEND,
ROBERT MOLLOY (1906-1977).

CONTENTS

THE LETTERS
(1971-1977)
OF
ROBERT MOLLOY

Preface

PREFACE

Robert Molloy was a dear friend, an excellent correspondent and a brilliant writer. We engaged in a fruitful and meaningful correspondence in 1971, and continued writing each other, at regular intervals, until his death in 1977. The near six-year period may not have been long; however, it was intense, and we got to know one another very well. Although I never met Molloy en chair et en os, I felt as though I knew him as one knows a best friend. We called each other several times on the phone, and I will never forget the poignant conversation we had when Molloy called me on 18 September 1976 to express his heartfelt sympathy, shortly after my beloved father had died. After such a heart-rending experience, the memory of his comforting, friendly and meaningful words and sagacious philosophical comments will never leave me.

The last letter Molloy wrote me was dated, 25 January 1977, and post-marked the following day. He died one day later, 27 January 1977, and when I read of his death in the New York *Times,* 28 January 1977, I wrote the following letter to Marion Molloy, his widow.

Dear Mrs. Molloy:

I just read about Robert's death in the NYT, and I am heartbroken and terribly distressed. A great sense of personal loss is immediate, and I truly feel inadequate to express my true feelings.
You well know that he was a very good friend of

mine, and friendship and loyalty, integrity and love never die. There has been, over the years, much affection in the friendship. Affection for his warm and personable nature, his many acts of kindness (he recently called me when my own father died), and his literary work. And equally as important--there was respect. In his meritorious example, we are all left better for his having lived.

Please accept my deepest sympathies, Mrs. Molloy. If there is anything I can do personally, please feel that you can call on me.

Yours most sincerely,
Mel B. Yoken

I received Molloy's last letter shortly after I read the obit in the *Times*. I was obviously deeply shaken and somewhat traumatized as I read his words, especially those about a future life, religion and resolutions. In spite of these profound and perhaps prophetic words and thoughts, Molloy, as always, retained his witty and linguistic propensities.

He was a veritable Renaissance man if ever that Homo sapiens lived. After all, he loved music, languages, the arts, and he was forever the scholar par excellence always in pursuit of what was the truth. Most important, perhaps, was his deep-rooted love for people, and he always showed that side to me.

Robert Molloy liked to write letters; he expressed this feeling to me both when he wrote to--and spoke with--me.

His letters, for which modern-day historians, scholars and the general-reader will be grateful, run an extremely wide-ranging gamut. They offer the reader brilliant and coruscating *aperçus* of a writer, his oeuvre and his epoch. The letters are always exciting, varied and, in one word, invaluable.

The reader will find that I have never intruded in the sacrosanctity of these letters with editorial comments, annotations or personal opinions. Titles of books, plays, poems and songs, when noted in a foreign language, have not been translated; however, for a better comprehension of the text itself, all Latin, French and Italian tags, words, aphorisms and expressions are translated at the end of each letter. I translated the French, and my colleague, Giulio Massano, a professor in the Department of Foreign Literature and Languages at Southeastern Massachusetts University, has most ably assisted me by translating the Latin and Italian. I am most grateful for his expert and friendly assistance.

Throughout the letters, Molloy refers to many authors, and a good number of political figures, singers and entertainers. The reader will have no particular trouble in identifying them, even though they are occasionally referred to only by the first or last name. Other references such as Cindy, refer to my wife; b.w. (beautiful wife), to his wife, Marion Molloy; and Tillier, to Claude Tillier, a French writer of the nineteenth century and subject of my doctoral dissertation, and later my book published by Twayne. Sun refers to the New York *Sun,* and the word "perles" which he usually does not underline, is a French word for errors which are often ridiculous and unrefined, in nature.

Molloy was, as a proofreader, an excellent speller. There are, however, throughout the letters, a very few misspellings which I have not corrected nor added [sic]. Dots of ellipses, when they appear, are in Molloy's original letters. All letters and postcards are presented, therefore, as they were received; no letters were eliminated.

Letters can help restore the flavor and feeling of an era or a certain period. Molloy's letters do that, and more. They seem to be destined for publication, for they are simply mesmerizing, splendiferous and important nuggets of information and comments about and by one man who will most certainly be remembered for his literary production which, like a fascinating conversation, rings agreeably and delectably well with any reader.

I have added, after all the letters, a most interesting letter in French (with English translation) sent Robert Molloy by Louise Lévêque, the daughter of Jean Talva, nom de plume of the French translator of Molloy's *Pride's Way*. Finally, the reader will find, at the end of the book, a delightful memoir written by Marion Molloy, dedicated to the honor and memory of her husband. Both the letter (and accompanying translation) and memoir will, most certainly, help the reader appreciate more fully the life and work of the great man and writer, Robert Molloy.

Finally, my personal thanks to Charles D.P. Seggelin, Faculty-Staff-Resource-Center Software Chief of SMU, who patiently helped me out to prepare the manuscript for its final printing. His computer expertise contributed greatly to the preparation of this book.

Mel B. Yoken
July 1988

Letters of Robert Molloy

Paramus, N.J.
May 21, 1971

Dear Professeur Yoken,

I am deeply apologetic about my failure to answer your very pleasant letter. In extenuation, may I say that I had a coronary late in December and that moving my affairs downstairs for a couple of months put a good many letters (and bills) astray. I am just getting my head above paper.

I don't care much for *Uneasy Spring*. After my first book, for which I have the prejudice that usually favors the firstborn, I like *An Afternoon in March* and *A Multitude of Sins*. Perhaps I like the last best. I am not a good judge and I never reread my work.

I was early influenced by many writers. Technically I have learned from Maugham. I should say that *Pride's Way* owes a bit to *Cranford* and *Tartarin de Tarascon*.

At present I am translating a Spanish work on Peru and earning my living as a copy editor at the *Daily News*. For recreation my wife and I have been reading French to each other every evening. We have just begun to re-acquaint ourselves with *Le Père Goriot*. I shall probably not write any more fiction at my age I am too conventional, I suppose. I do think about a commonplace book and have tinkered with a volume of childhood reminiscences. Let me say that I envy you your profession. Thank you for letting me know that someone still reads the stuff I wrote years ago. It was nice to hear from you.

Most cordially
Robert Molloy

Paramus, N.J.
August 1, 1972

Dear Dr. Ycken:

Of course a writer is always happy to know that someone with an impressive background likes his work. I enjoyed writing *Pound Foolish* but do not think it one of my best. It seems a little contrived and a bit naive to me now--this as a glance, for I assure you I don't re-read my novels. But please don't be influenced by my opinion! I'll be happy to know the results of your discussion of the novel.

Pride's Way was the most successful of my fiction but I think I prefer *An Afternoon in March*. Of the Charleston trilogy, perhaps *A Multitude of Sins* is the most smartly--I don't say brilliantly--written.

There are two counts against my doing anything in fiction now. One, I am out of the market and a middle-brow novelist can only be published successfully now if he has a market. The other count is that I am recovering slowly but surely from open heart surgery and don't feel very ambitious. A novel is a tremendous physical effort for me

I think you would love Charleston in the early spring. The significant remains are limited enough to see in a couple of weeks, superficially at least, and the flowers are very beautiful... in some ways. The city is like the Boston of *The Late George Apley*. I trust you share my admiration for Marquand at his best. He overdid his theme and echoed himself and his flashbacks became a sort of involuntary alteration, like Dr. Jekyll's.

9

Thanks for your interest and kind invitation of which I'll certainly take advantage if I happen to be up that way.

Sincerely
Robert W. Molloy

Paramus, N.J.
November 4, 1972

My dear Dr. Yoken,

Of course I am happy to sign the two books; however, they have felt the tooth of time and of <u>imber edax</u>.
Everyone has a stained book or two that happened to be on the windowsill or near an open window.
It would be nice to meet you and have a talk about mutual tastes. I imagine we must have several. I envy your occupation--I am a catch-as-catch-can linguist myself and respect all those who do better.
Pride's Way received a good deal of praise in 1945 and a few incidental honors--Southern Women's literary something-or-other and so forth. The book was a Literary Guild selection! And there were about 600,000 copies distributed. The trade sale was about 35,000 and as you know American publishers do not keep books in print so it was soon remaindered. There was an English edition of about 10,000 copies, and there were translations into French, Danish Norwegian and Swedish--<u>comprise la Scandinavie</u> as the copyright notices used to say. The French translation was clever--Gombo was used for the Negro dialect. The dear old lady who did the job, however, rendered "good and tired" as <u>bon et fatigué</u>, something like <u>la dernière chemise de l'amour</u>.
My present position at the *Daily News* is that of a copy editor, or copyreader as we usually call it. I translate bad journalese into something resembling English, avoid libel and errors of fact, and write headlines. It is an occupation I do not exactly cherish, as I have never had printer's ink in my veins and the triviality of so much I have

11

to deal with appals me. Anyway, I am going to retire at the end of next month, on the eve of my 67th birthday, after which I expect to loaf and invite my soul for whatever years are left. There are a lot of things I haven't time or energy for now, especially since my surgery, although I've almost recovered my full energy.

To return to your question about the publication figures, my later books did rather poorly. One was serialized in a women's magazine but only about 10,000 copies were sold and although *The Other Side of the Hill* was sold to a paperback house the figures were small and the payments exiguous. Only one of my books--*An Afternoon in March*--went into a second edition. This puts me in the company of Conrad Aiken, who said it was his second editions that were rare. Critical success has been small, although I've had the pleasure of being praised for little things that I had liked myself. Still it was like Mme. de Sevigné's apartment--que tout le monde admire mais que personne ne veut louer. So I cherish an occasional letter and appreciation--they keep me from feeling that I have suffered the fate of Beerbohm's Enoch Soames.

I have sometimes winced at the fluency of unsuccessful writers. Being unoccupied seems to be doing the same thing to me if the way this letter runs on is any indication. So I'll close it.

You could do me a favor sometime if occasion offers: I'd like to find a recording of Mallarmé's *L'Après-midi*. A dear old friend of ours was making a tape of it for me once, but she became so indignant at what seemed to her to be vague nonsense that she did not finish...

Thank you always for your very good wishes.
Veuillez agréer, Monsieur, mes sentiments les plus distingués (if that is right).

Robert W. Molloy

distinguées (?). Ma mémoire vieillit

Imber edax: Destructive storm

Comprise la Scandinavie: Including Scandinavia

Good and tired: épuisé [in French]

La dernière chemise de l'amour: The last shirt of love (for the last shift of love).

Que tout le monde admire mais que personne ne veut louer: That every one likes but nobody wants to rent it.

Paramus, N.J.
December 8, 1972

Dear Mr. Yoken,

You must think I am rude--but the package you sent on November just reached me yesterday.

It was very kind of you to send the records of Mallarmé, which I've enjoyed just once. This weekend I'll put them on tape and return them promptly. I shall also return the rare envelope--forsan et haec olim meminisse iuvabit!

The Boston Globe supplement is very lively and my wife and I and my sister-in-law will get a lot of pleasure from it.

I appreciate the fact that you are busy, and feel ashamed that I've put you to so much trouble about the Mallarmé records.

We (My wife and I) are both about to retire. I shall catch up on my reading and piano playing (I hope) and perhaps write a non-fiction book about my brother and me as little boys. Family snapshots and so forth. Possibly I have already told you of this project.

We have been watching *Cousine Bette* on TV. Very melodramatic in that form, a little bit of the penny dreadful about it. Once I read all Balzac's fiction--40 volumes--and I regret to say that although I am a Francophile, I am not a Balzacian. Are you? Quot homines tot sententiae--no one reads Anatole France now but he delighted my early years.

I'll wish you a very Merry Christmas and happy New

14

Year. Again very heartfelt thanks.

Yours most cordially
Robert W. Molloy

_____

Forsan et haec olim meminisse iuvabit!: Perhaps it will be helpful to remember the past!

Quot homines tot sententiae: There are as many opinions as there are human beings!

Paramus, N.J.
January 1st [1973]

Dear Dr. Yoken: Misplaced your home address so this to you at the University. Thanks very much indeed for your fine French letter of good wishes.

I have not returned the readings because we found that Christmas mail was so slow and so carelessly handled but you need not be uneasy about them as I'll put them in the mail this week. I have retired and can now loaf and invite my soul. Happy New Year to you.

Cordially
Robert Molloy

Paramus, N.J.
November 10, 1974

Cher Docteur,

Gavisus sum ut Latinam intellegas! I find very few
friends nowadays who can swap tags.

It was indeed good to hear from you. There must be
something in extra-sensory perception--just the other day I
was looking at a recording of *L'Après-midi* which I bought
in Paris (the poem is not complete) and I remembered your
kind loan of French records. It does seem a long time ago.
We went to France and Italy in 1973, a year after my open
heart surgery. I got along very well in French, by the way--
even managing to change trains upon the advice of a clerk
in Nîmes, meridional accent and all.

It is certainly flattering that someone still reads
Pride's Way. Tell it not in Gath but the people were
modeled on my grandmother, great-aunt, parents, etc. But I
heard from people everywhere that their own aieux were
just like that; even a Roumanian Jewish friend told me they
were just like his grandmother and great-aunt. Habent sua
fata libelli--I'm glad mine has at least one loyal fan.

I left Charleston when I was twelve and did not return
until a year after that first novel appeared. The incidents, by
the way, are largely imaginary--only the quarrel of the two
old ladies was fact. But some people saw themselves. They
did not seem to mind with the exception of my late uncle.

An Afternoon in March is in a way my favorite of the
books I have written. All my later books were more or less
limited editions! But that one had a second. I cannot find an
extra copy so I am sending you as a loan the only copy of
the second edition--a rarity, as Conrad Aiken said of his

17

second editions. Please return it at your convenience. It is based on a famous murder in the 1880's and I had the 35mm transcript of the testimony from the local paper. I was abused in the Charleston *News and Courier* after the book appeared; one of the things they said was that the book was a mere copy of the testimony, which made me laugh as I wrote nearly all the court scene myself, following only the legal points.

I retired in late December of 1972 and have never regretted it. I spend my leisure practicing the piano and struggling to learn Greek--the motivation does not seem strong enough and I learn slowly. There was a plan to rewrite Scott's *Bride of Lammermoor* but I have only the notes and outline of that. As for the childhood reminiscences, well, I doubt that anyone would read them and publication is difficult these days. I've written some bits and captioned the snapshots. I seem to have recovered from the cacoethes scribendi.

I trust your dissertation on Tillier will have a great popular success. The Hackensack library buys every one of the Twayne publications and I shall whoop it up.

Authors disappear. No one reads Anatole France now although we loved him. As for Loti... There is a radio program from Paris, relayed through the New York city station, called *French in the Air*. Lately they have been discussing Alphonse Allais, a humorist of the turn of of the century.

By the way, I saw a bit of Tarascon. We also were shown Daudet's Moulin. I love the south of France. All but the mistral, that is. Parisians, too, were very nice to us. They have as you well know a bad name among Americans, but we found only one instance of abruptness even and that was from an aged shopkeeper who did not have what we wanted.

Otherwise, in the words of Guillaume Apollinaire, <u>les jours s'en vont je demeure</u>. Bientôt j'aurai soixante neuf ans.

By all the means let me hear from you again before too many moons.

Yours ever,
Robert

P.S. I don't think the sale of *An Afternoon in March* was helped by the frightful cover jacket. By the way, the lawyer Mr. Montague was based on Octavus Roy Cohen's father, Asher Cohen, a great criminal lawyer.

Cher Docteur: Dear Doctor

Gavisus sum ut Latinam intellegas!: I rejoice that you understand latin!

Aïeux: ancestors

Habent sua fata libelli: Pamphlets will receive their just rewards.

Cacoethes scribendi.: Incurable passion for writing

Moulin: windmill

Les jours s'en vont je demeure: Days go by, I remain.

Bientôt j'aurais soixante-neuf ans: Soon I will be sixty-nine

Paramus, N.J.
December 19, 1974

Dear Mel,

I was holding my fire in replying to your last letter. Your opinion of my book was very flattering. I don't deserve it but I warm my hands at it.

I do not attend MLA tauroboliums because I am not a scholar. But I'd like to see you--my fans are an endangered species!(*). I suggest you call me at the above number when you arrive the evening of the 27th. Conditions may be such on the last Saturday before Christmas that we'll have to jockey for a table--but they may not. I am only 45 minutes by express bus from the bus terminal.

Answering your question about my books, I am inclined to put *Pound Foolish* fairly low. *A Multitude of Sins* was better. *An Afternoon in March* may have sold 4000 copies. I was what I call an overhead author--one who helps to keep the salesmen and editors busy and fill out the catalogue. I do not feel at all proud of *Uneasy Spring*. Two novels with a partial Charleston background, *The Reunion* and *The Other Side of the Hill* (believe the latter had a character from Charleston in it) were good jobs but few people were attracted. It is a long time since people last wrote to me about any of these novels.

Like you I am distressed at the plight of humanity and the callousness of those who have full bellies. To paraphrase Emerson, what we need is a a moral equivalent for religion. (Not Emerson, but William James).

Your "écriture" is perfectly clear. Mine is difficult for a lot of people. I comfort myself by cultivating the feeling that they read letter by letter, like children.

I'll look forward to hearing from you. We do not get to sleep before midnight--don't hesitate to call late.

Yours ever,
Robert

(*) that is tactlessly expressed--not the real reason

MLA: Modern Language Association

Tauroboliums:sacrifice in which the faithful were bathed with the blood of the immolated bull

Ecriture: writing

Paramus, N.J.
January 11, 1975

Dear Mel,

I enjoyed your letter. Poland Springs is probably a bit
cool for my ancient circulation but you make it sound
inviting.

Your abrogation program is a corollary to the motto on
sundials (horas non numero nisi serenas, in case you've
forgotten). The future is longer and more threatening for
younger people. I am nearer to saying inveni portum and I
don't mean that to violate your motto. In some respects I
have seen the world at its best.

I go into New York about three times a year. As I have
given up the theatre as too expensive and too unrewarding
and detest the current course of movies the only thing I
miss is the 42nd Street library and conditions there are
crowded. I do live in one of the Saharas of the Beaux-Arts-
-can't obtain a copy of Greville's diary or a Latin Vulgate or
the second and third volumes of Bryant's life of Pepys.

I have not usually had trouble with getting novels
finished. I liked to think them out a bit in advance. I wrote
the last 75 printed pages of one in three and a half working
days. It was like automatic writing, end spurt or something.
But of course with a scholarly work it would be different,
especially if I had to please a pre-editor as you have had to
do. My unsuccessful (unprinted) novel about Robert
Schumann cost me two years of research and a year of
writing and my publishers were correct in declining it. I
fiddled around with another long semi-autobiographical
novel but shelved it more than two years ago. There was so
much material. I may still write my book of boyhood

22

sketches with old snapshots as a point d'appui and carry out my intention of revamping Scott's *Bride of Lammermoor* to make it a bit more easy for modern readers. Scott was ill and dictated it and it shows the flaws one might expect.

But I am no Flaubert (that's modesty for you). Seven years was too much for *Madame B.* and perhaps Nietzsche was right when he said that it smelled of the lamp. But the scene at the fair has never been rivaled, in my opinion, for virtuosity--action on three stages.

How would P.G. Wodehouse translate into French? His stock of new metaphors used to be inexhaustible and his style a delight. Like all old men he has been repeating himself many years, more's the pity. I ask because I collect odd translations--*Ferdinand the Bull* into Latin, the *Alice* books into Latin, French, Italian and Spanish, and so forth.

As for my own old age, je deviens bavard à soixante-neuf ans. So I'll preserve some random thoughts for another letter. I'll just add that maybe we can get together on your grounds or mine and that I hope so, before I am taken to the jardin des refroidis.

Yours for a quiet life,
Robert

Horas non numero nisi serenas: I don't count the hours unless they are happy ones.

Inveni portum: I found the harbor (refuge)

Beaux-arts: Fine arts

Point d'appui: Illustrative point, basis

Je deviens bavard à soixante-neuf ans: I become talkative at 69

Jardin des refroidis: Garden of dead (and cold) bodies

23

Paramus, N.J.
February 4, 1975

Dear Prof,

Thanks for your letter. And thanks, belatedly, for putting my "works" in the SMU library. If I ever am reincarnated as Enoch Soames I'll look there first.

It's good to know that your book is in the works. Parting with a ms. is a little like seeing a loved one off to the wars but the strain lightens little by little.

Your course in practical French sounds great. I wish age, distance and ignorance did not prevent me from enrolling.

We'll get up to see your university if the Arabs give us a break. My only experience of teaching, by the way, was one semester in elementary journalism to replace a friend and teacher at N.Y.U., and two semesters in charge of a course in novel writing at Columbia's School of General Studies. I enjoyed it and the youngsters (and some older) thought I had put on a good show. Not that you can teach anybody how to write fiction! When André Maurois told Alain that he was going to be a writer Alain made him copy out *Le Rouge et le Noir* in longhand.

As for the uses of education, except for the enlargement of the personality, I have become a bit of a curmudgeon in my dotage. You have beaten me to it--there is just too much ad hoc educating which is only what Everett Dean Martin, in the 1920s, called training.

My French must make you squirm. I can read almost anything but my ear is poor and I don't speak or write well.

Obviously the <u>Bibliothèque Rose</u> did not include a translation of *Ferdinand the Bull*. My children came along at just the right time for it. It is a little masterpiece, written in forty-five minutes by a publisher's editor and magnificently illustrated by Robert Lawson. Get a copy from the junior room of the nearest public library. It is not scatological or stercoraceous (which cannot be said for some of the children's books I see reviewed week after week).

I detest contemporary fiction and just do not read it, and I don't see skin movies either. Not that I am a Puritan to that extent but that the people and their problems do not interest me, beginning with Portnoy. I have had a generally happy sex life on the quiet side and think all these frustrated people need what my old boss (an Englishman) suggested--a kick in the pratt.

By the way, do you have access to the works of Banville? The poem *Nous n'irons plus au bois* has been tormenting me and I can't find my copy. If you would transcribe it--about ten lines--I'd be grateful. I think it's in a volume titled *Orientales*. Don't make a big effort. The New York Public Library has discarded the copy that used to be on the reading room shelves. I wrote the poem out this morning but I'm not one hundred per cent sure I haven't left out something or invented some phrases. He was, if you have forgotten, one of the Parnassiens.

I do not, unfortunately, make good use of my leisure. Deus mihi haec otia fecit--but unfortunately has not furnished the energy I'd like to have. I try to tell myself Courage... le diable est mort, but I'm not sure.

Your use of the word onus reminds me of my favorite pun. Schopenhauer was bothered by two old crones who talked incessantly on the landing outside his door and in a fit of temper he threw one of them down the stairs. A court ordered him to pay her regular damages--monthly, or weekly. When he heard that she had died he wrote in his diary

Obit anus; abit Onus.

With which happy thought I'll leave you for the time being. The best of luck with your new class and your book.

R.

Ad hoc: Special

Bibliothèque Rose: A well known French edition for children

Nous n'irons plus au bois: We won't go to the woods anymore (It has become a nursery rhyme. Its origin is far different and refers to the fact that the Red Light District in Paris was called Le bois (The wood), due to the fact that the houses of ill repute displayed in front of their door a laurel bush. King Louis the XIIth (1250 AD) ordered all the whorehouses closed and the laurels cut.)

Deus mihi haec otia fecit:God gave me this time for leasure

Courage... le diable est mort: Cheer up... The devil is dead

Onus: burden

Obit anus; abit Onus: the aged person dies; the burden goes away.

Dear Mel,

We are very sorry that your telephone call didn't reach us. Something must have gone wrong, as we were both at home and wide awake.

Thank you for all the trouble you went to in getting the Banville verses and for that copy of his letter. His handwriting was beautiful and very clear.

I am glad to know that one of the younger generation doesn't automatically sneer at Banville. I don't know many of his poems but the lauriers is one of my favorites--music and imagery. I had composed a number of words, or rather my unconscious had done it, when I was trying to recall the words. So your search got me off the hook.

So I am known at Brown University, too? Don't encourage them to include *Pound Foolish*, of which I am not proud. The non-fiction book was one of the Cities Series, with drawings by E.H. Suydam.

My younger son was a disc jockey (classical) in Houston for a while. He is a violinist in the Houston Symphony and he got the radio job on the strength of his good ear for foreign musical titles, French included. It's because he has absolute pitch, as does his older brother the pianist. When they were little boys they could sing Mozart arias in Italian just from hearing them on a phonograph.

No Frenchman could possibly rival the late Van Wyck Brooks for cacography--though that's not quite the right word, as his hand <u>looked</u> pretty enough. What he <u>meant</u> reminded me of the story about the Irishman who said that he didn't know whether to laugh or cry--he had just had a

27

letter from his brother and "if this is an o̲ the poor fellow shot himself." My father and two older brothers wrote copperplate hands.

The snow did its bit here. All gone now except for a patch or north sides of houses etc. My wife detests snow because of the driving danger but even she admitted that the 8 inches we had was beautiful.

I've read the music festival program with interest. It looks like a good show. You are not teaching French diction or did I miss your name? Most Americans sing French the way Goldowsky speaks English. If as well... As for the Italians... Je reste muet. (Is that right?)

Always a pleasure to hear from you. Avoid the flu.

Yours ever,
Robert

Je reste muet: I don't say a word (literally: I keep mute).

Dear Mel,

We arrived Saturday afternoon after a spotty trip--it rained from Wilmington N.C. to Cape Charles Va. without once letting up. Southern gardens from south Virginia down were beautiful, although the great Magnolia Gardens were a little past their height and the oleanders were just budding. Charleston is a fantastically built city. Marion didn't see as much of it as I had hoped--she had been there only once before--because, as a big fish in a little pool, I attracted a good deal of inviting. Not the self-styled aristocrats, but some very interesting people. And of course I had to sacrifice on the family altar.

It is still winter here--my garden hasn't progressed a bit since we left on the first of the month.

The seed catalogs are a great temptation and a snare and a delusion but we always come back for more.

Sorry to hear that you feel poorly. Maybe they'll have to blow out your Eustachian tube. Anyway, I hope the difficulty clears up. In my dotage I seem to have inherited my mother's immunity to colds of all kinds although I picked up a bad one in Rome two years ago.

We listen only to news broadcasts and Channel 13 (public tv) shows. The ads are disgusting and I hate to eat dinner with an accompaniment of laxative and hemorrhoids discussions. The politicians are pretty bad. On the whole the newsmen are reasonably skeptical but TV is not designed for the intelligent. We often wonder that even such a middlebrow affair as the CBS news broadcast can entertain such moronic advertisements. My theory is that they consider their listeners feeble-minded, which for the most part they are.

My favorite French mistranslation is La Dernière Chemise de l'Amour. But in the German translation of Hamlet the line about sledded Polacks on the ice the translator made it <u>Streitaxt</u> (pole ax, if you don't know German) and had the king slamming in into the ice. <u>Traduttore</u>, <u>traditore</u>...

Oddly enough, I didn't get any crab soup--the times it was on the list I wanted something else and was afraid it would spoil my appetite.

I see that you know Portuguese, which I consider badly spelled Spanish. I had to read a good deal of it once, which I did by intuition as I've never studied it.

My cat was so glad to have us back and to be out of the kennel that she is right now hindering my efforts to write by lying on my desk and ruffling the papers. She is tawny and white and we named her Fulvia--after her coloring, not after Mark Antony's wife.

Some detestable person put her out to forage when she was a kitten and she bummed her way around the neighborhood for about six months avoiding cars and dogs until we couldn't resist adopting her.

Good wishes to your brother on his syndicated feature. The sample you sent was very amusing.

Somewhere I have a clipping of *Peanuts* in French. I'll send it along when I clear my desk...

Valete,
Robert

Your handwriting is all right!

La Dernière Chemise de l'Amour: The Last Shirt of Love (for the *Love's Last Shift*).

Traduttore, traditore: translator, traitor

Valete: be well

Paramus, N.J.
May 12, 1975

Dear Mel,

I was happy to have your photograph--even with the beard it gives me a clearer idea of your personality. I grew one, years ago before it was stylish. My hair was blond, my eyebrows black and the beard red. I got rid of it. I also once had a mustache and my wife's aunt said it made me look like a tough Irish bartender.

We have has a reluctant spring here--Saturday and yesterday very mild and pleasant. Now it is raining. My cherry tree (Japanese) was in fullest bloom Saturday. Today the petals are falling. <u>Alas, that spring</u>...

I have about decided to give up listening to the TV news. My wife likes to have it going at dinnertime. I usually take my coffee and dessert into my room to avoid a squinting vulgarian named Pat Collins and the sportscaster. I think I shall give up the "Krankheit" program too. I simply can't tolerate those ads much longer. Fortunately we have WNET.

You are right about the relaxing of all morality in government. Of course Harding was a good-natured pushover for crooks in office, and Eisenhower had his Sherman Adams. Truman had some bad company but the man himself was true blue. Read Merle Miller's book about him. It will amuse you and do you good.

I'm glad you find Groucho a comfort. My wife re-reads Jane Austen. I listen to music, play the piano an hour a day, and have started lessons with a vocal coach. At 69 there isn't a great deal of voice left but he will improve my legato and enunciation. I meant to say that my wife also reads whodunits which I do not enjoy. I have lost my taste for nearly all fiction. Recently I re-read *The Mayor of Casterbridge* and enjoyed it. I used to be a Hardy fan by never got around to the lesser novels and don't think I ever shall.

It is surprising to find out when your are on the last lap that a great many things do not have the overwhelming significance they once had. I don't mean that one's zest for life is any feebler, necessarily, but the emphasis is different. I do become a bit ruled up over the flood of illiteracies in the Times! Literacy is dead.

Etymology fascinates me still, my appetite is good and quite catholic and I enjoy my night's sleep and amusing dreams, mad though some of them are. Open heart surgery is now three years behind me but it has affected my breath intake--diaphragm weakness, I suppose, so that I tire rather easily when gardening or exercising. I wish there were more opportunities for good conversation, but my friends are out on Long Island or in New England and I live in a blue collar neighborhood--agreeable folk but not precisely witty or inspired.

Senator Buckley wants us to bomb Cambodia because of their seizing a U.S. ship. Great people, the Buckleys. A pest on <u>toute la smalah</u>.

Write when you have a moment and the urge.

Robert

Toute la smalah: all the family

33

Dear Mel,

Thanks for the W.C account. I can only reply with the story about the young Frenchman on his lune de miel. He had worked out a code with his brother by which he would report progress. Unfortunately for the plan the first telegram was opened by his father. It read "C'est 13 et 3.."The father wrote back, "Si c'est 13 et 3, c'est 9." No doubt you've heard it, these many years.

We had a couple of steamy days and today it has rained since noon, the prediction being thunder showers. I have never had any faith in weather predictions. Any farmer with a rheumatic toe can do better.

As between Buckley and Bella I prefer Bella.

Public TV--Channel 13 here--is the only escape from the horrors that make us both shudder. I do not understand people any longer. On the CBS 6 o'clock news they invariably have five minutes about some horrible "singing organization"--never the arrival of a great European orchestra of anything like that.

Of course we are victims of our inventions. The telephone is the curse of most people's lives. The airplane has made it possible to kill millions quickly. And someone once said that when printing became so cheap that a page of printed matter could be carelessly trampled, it signified a major loss to true culture. Well, I am within six months of the Biblical three score and ten and it won't matter to me so very much longer.

I do feel sorry for the young. As you say, they are being promised pie in the sky. Not getting it, they have no inner resources. I live in a superior blue collar neighborhood and all the neighbors' children openly detest reading. The bigger boys wander around all summer and every week end, playing one kind of ball game or another to kill time. I know nothing about their emotional or sex lives except through hearsay but apparently as in every thing else they get what they want, long before they are able to appreciate it. New bikes every year--I had one that lasted years and years. The boy across the street bought an amplifier to make the noises of his "combo" ten times as loud. He paid, I believe, $300 for it. His banjo, a cheap affair, cost him $144.

Speaking of music, I confess to being a complete longhair in this. Aside from a few popular songs of my childhood and earlier that amuse me I stick to the classics from Bach to Stravinsky--the extreme contemporary school does not interest me.

I confess that my first feeling about the Vietnam refugees was "what about Appalachia and the Indians and Negroes?" but my better self intervened. I think we'll absorb the influx without too much dislocation and after all their plight is largely of our making.

You mention Nathalie Sarraute. I have read almost nothing of the newer school of European novelists. In fact, I have rather lost interest in fiction. Read all you can now while you are on the sunny side of the valley. I lose myself in books of quotations, miscellaneous essays, and a bit of poetry. Conversation, when I can get it, amuses me; but most of my friends live at some distance and everyone is always too busy. The old custom of dropping in on your neighbors in the evening has died in my lifetime. And the people around here cannot really converse. Besides, it keeps them from mowing the lawn or watching the great grey plague, as I once characterized TV.

35

As a horrible example of what goes on in this Sahara of the Beaux Arts, we were trying to find the source of the byword, "Home, James, and don't spare the horses." No luck. My wife mentioned this to a friend who has a clerical position in the local high school and she volunteered to ask those in the English department. She came back with the suggestion that it probably was said by <u>Henry James</u>. As William McFee used to say, "Stand back--give me air!".

And the music chairman of the same school, at a choral concert, was guilty of telling the audience that the *Carmina Catulli* were settings of the poems of a "Roman nobleman", and that the *Carmina Burana* were settings of medieval poems found in a <u>Spanish</u> monastery. What do you think? I was going to write him a snooty letter but as with the New York Times it is useless. The mistakes just keep on multiplying.

Do you know about the baritone who was singing the part of the toreador in *Carmen*? When he came to the words, "qu'un oeil noir te regarde" he frowned furiously. The director asked him why he did this and he replied, "Mais c'est pour imiter le regard du taureau."

Cura ut valeas,
Robert

Lune de miel: Honeymoon

C'est 13 et 3 (C'est treize et trois): It is 13 and 3. The pronunciation is the same as "c'est très étroit", which means it's very narrow.

Si c'est 13 et 3 c'est neuf (Si c'est treize et trois, c'est neuf): If it is 13 and 3, then it is 9. The pronunciation is the same as "si c'est très étroit c'est neuf", which means if it's very tight it new (neuf means both new and nine)

Qu'un oeil noir te regarde: A dark eyes stares at you

Mais c'est pour imiter le regard du taureau: But it's to imitate the bull's glance

Cura ut valeas: take care of yourself

Dear Mel,

We enjoyed your good letter, and are grateful for the beautiful Chinese cookbook. A store has opened in the neighborhood and Marion will be able to make up some of the recipes. Thanks also for the bicentennial papers. An ambitious job.

I am not close to academic groves of any sort now and confess ignorance about the Middlebury French program. I am glad some school stresses something other than management, investing, and supermarket operation. I also applaud their attitude toward freeloading politicians.

We love Vermont and New Hampshire on the strength of brief motel stays while aiming for Maine.

Bella Abzug does rasp one's sensibilities a bit but I think her heart is under the right layer of blubber. I cannot abide the arrogant Buckleys and as a long-term agnostic I despise their conservatism, Vatican induced.

If we were a bit younger we might think of sponsoring or adopting one of the refugees. A delicate, fire-boned race. I first learned about them from Burton Holmes' travelogues in the 1920s. It was Indochina then, of course.

We too have had some nice weather but today it was cloudy and humid and now we are finishing up a thunderstorm that began about six o'clock.

Do not be too optimistic about the future of freedom. They are chipping away at the foundations, as you say, hour by hour. McCarthyism is not dead.

A favor: would you or any of your colleagues know who popularized or coined the expression déjà vu? We have been trying to trace it for a librarian friend.

And is there a book of French puzzles etc., like the rebuses exchanged by Voltaire and Frederick of Prussia, like:

$$\frac{P}{venez} \quad à \quad \frac{ci}{100}$$

Trust you are aestivating agreeably.

Robert

$$\frac{P}{venez} \quad à \quad \frac{ci}{100}$$: Venez souper à Sans-Souci [in French]. Have dinner in Sans-Souci

Déjà vu: Formerly seen

Paramus, N.J.
July 15, 1975

Dear Mel,

Orthography is a matter for pedants, after all. And titles of books are certainly the easiest kind of thing to screw up.

What is Sloan Wilson up to now? I haven't seen his name for a long while. But then I am out of touch.

New England summers are great and I envoy you your access to them. Too far to drive now--we used to go to Bar Harbor every September but it's a long trip with stops for us. I don't even consider the winters--too much effort to keep warm. The pictures are always beautiful.

We were recently in Columbia County for a couple of days with friends--near Massachusetts line. Years ago when my sons were little we owned a small house (shack would be more accurate) for about ten years. Nice brook with swimming hole, 2 1/4 acres, lots of planting left by the first owner. I was just a boy of 38 when we bought the place!

The Italian version of Goldilocks was much enjoyed. I had some copies made for the right people and am sending one to my friend Commendatore Faincullo of Uatsamarra U.

At home I was always called by my full name. Don't know why unless there was a foretaste of my forbidding personality. In the newspaper business it is taken for granted that everyone has a nickname. My wife calls me Robert. I once remarked that every Tom, Dick and Harry was named Bob.

As for autobiographical projects, some of my life has gone indirectly into fiction... background. The only exciting thing that ever happened to me was slamming the door and walking out (in the opposite order) while my pater was giving me a dressing down. I have planned but not executed a book of old snapshots and portraits with captions and comment and may do it yet. But I'm very lazy. I have also a commonplace book in mind, and a scheme for rewriting a Scott novel in more modern form.

Recently I have been having some vocal coaching with a young soprano of the City Opera Company. I said to her that I preferred to sing lieder and added that in my opinion an American who tried to sing French was just sticking his neck out. She disagreed. Once I played a French song-- a recording of course--sung by a good English tenor, Heddle Nash, for an old friend of ours who was born in France of American parents. "What language is he singing?" she asked me. What do you think?

I have no prejudice against good autobiographies. Some of the people who write them don't have any more excuse than I have, I suppose. Arnold Bennett's journal is a fascinating book but as a general thing writers don't tell enough about their work and the only climaxes in a writer's life are rejection slips. Some day I am going to read Jules Renard's *Journal*. I believe it's all about other people, generally waspish.

You know of course about the young French curé who had to pronounce the funeral eulogy for a young girl of the parish. He did all right until he got to the end and his peroration was "Elle a vécu en vierge; elle est morte en sainte."

A publisher wants me to translate a French medical guide but the pay is too small. Perhaps you know a translator who might be interested in a little hack work of the kind?

We have had some storm weather for a few days.

41

Sunday we came home from rain in the Poconos and had it most of the way. Sunny in Paramus, but the storm followed us and caught up at about 5 p.m. Meanwhile, unbeknownst to us, there had been a hurricane through part of Paramus and we had several phone calls asking if we were all right. It was the first we had heard of it!

Continue to enjoy your vacances. The years go very quickly after 35, and soon you begin to say, "It seems like yesterday" or "Good Lord, is it Christmas time again?"

Write when the spirit moves. And again thanks for the beautiful cookbook. I once met Mickey Hahn at publishers' teas--a few times. She would not remember me.

Grandson of my "guide" in the Garrigues has won first prize at the Conservatoire, violin. He is just 14. A nice little chap when I met him in 1973. The family is <u>gonflée d'orgueil</u> (my pidgin French).

Best to you,
Robert

Elle a vécu en vierge; elle est morte en sainte: She lived like a virgin, she died like a saint.[En sainte is a homonym for enceinte which means pregnant.]

Vacances: Vacation

Gonflée d'orgueil: Full of pride

Paramus, N.J.
July 29, 1975

Dear Mel,

We too have had nasty weather for a bit, but the last four days have been halcyon--if a little warm. I do not sleep well these summer nights in spite of my hypnotic discipline--the air chokes me up and my left sinus clogs. No doubt the pollutants and the cloud-seeding have something to do with the mugginess and determined precipitation. We avoided the hurricane--it was northwest of our part of Paramus and we knew nothing about it until people called up.

As a meteorologist you probably won't agree with me that the reason for the unreliable and inaccurate forecasting is the increased sophistication of the equipment. My theory is that this leads to too great qualification on the part of the operators--whereas in the old days (eheu fugaces) someone took a look at the barometer and the last five years' records and made his prediction. Having no all-day radio he was stuck with it until the next day's newspaper.

I am glad you keep your sense of humor. Interesting the literal-minded in Baudelaire... You might say quia est in eo virtus odorosa. I once tried to explain to an Italian copy editor--good linguist--the beauty of some of the lines in Canto V of the *Divine Comedy*--I said amor che a nullo amato amar perdona sounded like a sob. He couldn't capire. Fortunately les sons et les parfums will continue to tourner dans l'air du soir.

I'm afraid most of the calembours and gaffes I know are common property. There are some good Latin ones, chiefly from Cicero who as you know was a great kidder.

43

Years ago the library in N.Y. had a collection of his japes but it has disappeared and I cannot recall the title or the name of the editor.

Our garden doesn't prosper--<u>too much rain</u>. The lettuce is stunted, the carrots are all tops, the beets the size of marbles. <u>Too much rain</u>. Our flowers, however, have done well. You are right about the wildlife. We have rabbits and chipmunks and a neighboring cat or two. The dogs are usually leashed and do not transgress. A skunk pays us a visit every evening and fills the air with homely cheer. Your family dinner sounds like a good old-fashioned beano.

The beaches, the forests, the meadows--everything is proof nowadays that only man is vile, as the poet said. We live on a dead end street. Slobs park for various purposes and throw their beer cans on the grass. I once defined a condominium as any lovers' lane on Sunday morning in the days before the pill. Paramus is facing the threat of high-rise housing. When that begins, good night!

I could grouse about the small annoyances of advancing age--energy lowered, occasional feeling that nothing matters very much, increasing Philistinism. An extra cocktail makes me sleepy and it is ten years now that I have been limited to three eggs a week--I who used to eat at least two every day of my life. I don't go quite so far as to say <u>La chair est triste, hélas, et j'ai lu tous les livres</u>, but sometimes I know what the poet meant. I wish I were 68 again.

I have been reading *The Brain Revolution* by Marilyn Ferguson, a summing up for popular consumption of all that is down and suspected about that blob of caseous matter. Perhaps I shall add mind control to my hobbies-- after hypnotism. I have long been appalled by the certainty that most of us use about one tenth of our capacities.

Friends of ours are going to the south of France for a vacation. I envy them no end. The Garrigues is just my sort of place, except for the mistral. The air! The flowers! The easy-going people, including the old loafers who tip their hats to you as you go past their bench, the little working-class restaurants where a sumptuous lunch is cooked up by the wife of the owner and a word of praise in poor French makes her smile happily. The 14th century plumbing is not more than adequate but que voulez-vous? A good place to _feignasser_, the south. An old friend of mine used to say Avec de la patience on peut enculer une mouche. Those people work hard but they seem able to sit around and drink in the sun.

Cura ut valeas
Robert

Eheu fugaces: How swiftly (time goes)

Quia est in eo virtus odorosa: Because there is in him a fragrant virtue.

Amor che a nullo amato amar perdona: Love that forgives even when it is not reciprocated. (Inferno, Dante)

les sons et les parfums: Sounds and fragrances

Tourner dans l'air du soir: flutter in the evening breeze

La chair est triste, hélas, et j'ai lu tous les livres: Flesh is sad, alas, and I have read all the books

Que voulez-vous?: What can we do? (Literally: What do you want?)

Feignasser: To fool around

Avec de la patience on peut enculer une mouche: With patience you could screw a fly.

45

Paramus, N.J.
August 27, 1975

Dear Professeur,

Thank you for the fine Paris print. They do things nicely, n'est-ce pas? Or as Sterne said, "They order these things better in France."

The "defaced" copy of P.W. goes to you under separate cover.

Your visit to Paris and the west sounds great. I have seen very little of France--Paris for a week, Uzès (in the Garrigues) for a week. I agree with you about Paris. London is fine but Paris is superb. We had been told that the French were snooty to Americans but had no such experiences. I thought once or twice they smiled at my French (and do not blame them.)

My people were from Alsace via Santo Domingo and Charleston--New Orleans. Their name was really Weiss but they were the business agents or something of the sort for the great St. Amand family, so when they came to the New World they assumed the greater name. Or have I already told you this?

I am not sure I could stand the elevation of the Pyrenees region as I have an enlarged heart as hangover from the years of valve trouble, and the 2000 and less feet in the Poconos is uncomfortable for me after a day or so.

If we ever have the good fortune to go to Paris again

we shall look up the hotel you stopped at. It cost us 90 francs a day at the Madeleine Plaza and that was two years and a half ago.

The thing in Paris that thrilled me the most, really, was the grave of Héloise and Abélard--not to mention the other resting places of the great in Père Lachaise. One of the odd things we saw there was a middle-aged lady, schoolmarm type, with a group of very young boys and girls. They were standing around Colette's tombstone and she was talking to them about "the great writer Colette." Not exactly for children, would you say?

We have had a great stroke of luck in N.Y.C. Radio station WNCN has returned after ten months. Some people telephoned them and <u>cried</u> into the telephone!

It was a terrible loss as the other "classical" stations have not the <u>métier</u>--something a little flat about their presentations and the actual broadcasting is not as brilliant although WNCN plays only recordings. Or should I use the word "flair"?

We have had some wretched weather--heat, rain, etc. My left nostril gets clogged by some allergy or other and wakes me up. From September 8 to 16 we shall be at Stone Harbor, on the New Jersey coast a little north of Cape May, and I hope to breathe normally there.

<u>A propos de bottes</u>, do you know what the librettist of *Thaïs* said when he was asked why he called the monk "Athanaël" instead of "Paphnuce" as in the novel? He explained that there were only two French words to rhyme with Paphnuce--<u>puce</u> and <u>prépuce</u>.

On which note I shall sign off. Happy to hear from you.

Yours ever,
Robert

N'est-ce-pas: Isn't it?
Métier: Profession
A propos de bottes: About boots
Puce: Flea
Prépuce: Foreskin

Stone Harbor, N.J
September 13, 1975

Stone Harbor is neat, quiet and airy. You can walk across the street without imperilling your neck. The surf is a bit rough for an aging Leander. I am eating too much! All the best.

Robert

Paramus, N.J.
September 20, 1975

Dear Mel,

I was away when your letter arrived. I enjoyed it. It made me feel happy to be enjoying retirement--the opening say you describe would have put me flat on my <u>dos</u>. But you are just half my age.

I am glad you enjoy my sense of the ridiculous. I do not usually quote my own gags but the recent death of Haile Selassie reminds me that I saw him in a parade and reported to my colleagues that he was "every half inch a king."

You sent me some samples of your brother's cartoon venture. Is he acquainted (I mean does he know the ropes!) with the field? I think the usual way is to place your feature in a newspaper or two--some of the Rhode Island ones might do--and then send the printed issues or facsimiles to syndicates. I also believe it is possible to syndicate oneself. Tell him, if he hasn't done so, to look in the Literary Market Place (Bowker) under "News Services and Feature Syndicates." There are a lot of them. But he ought to get a good book on free-lance writing and see what it says about selling daily or weekly features. I used to have a pleasant relationship with Norton Mockridge when we were on the World Telegram. Norton started an old-fashioned column, the kind in which readers send in their clippings, contributions and comments--and he made it go.

Amen to what you say about the politicos. Even the good ones are hokum specialists. The public just won't vote for the Stevensons. The *Osservatore* is right, even if it is published by a fascist organization (Molloy the agnostic

50

speaking).

Our fall is later here than yours. Some trees are just turning. I am torn between esthetic considerations and the awful feeling that once more I've got to get out in my back yard and gather them up. As we have virtually a quarter acre and are surrounded by trees I feel like the street cleaner in the Charlie Chaplin film when he saw the elephant coming. <u>Automne au ciel brumeux, aux horizons navrants</u>... A nice song by Faure, words, as I'm sure you know, by Silvestre.

Your line from Racine is a gem. I am very fond of <u>Mais la mort fuit encore sa grande âme trompée</u>, from *Mithridate*. I am fond of monosyllables myself but often in English they are like sledge-hammer blows. (I used to tell young writers and my few students to leave out adjectives-- same effect--as in Macbeth's soliloquy.)

Speaking again of politics, have you chanced to read *This Was Cicero* by H. J. Haskell (1936)? Things haven't changed a bit.

Thanks for the Russell Baker piece. He was at his best in that I think he writes too often, and tries too hard a good deal of the time.

I ran across an innocent bit in the *Reader's Digest*-- old copy. A man dined in a Chinese restaurant and got two fortune cookies for his dessert. He opened one and the slip of paper said "Hard work is the only secret of success." He opened the other and found the same message. "I hate a fortune cookie that nags," he said.

We were at the beach--believe I sent you a card. Water too rough and too much wind but we enjoyed ourselves. However, I was glad to get back to my wife's simple <u>cuisine</u>--her mother and grandmother were two of the best cooks that ever lived.

Some time ago I encountered a preface to the works of

Villon which said that his name was correctly pronounced
franswais villion. Is this correct, M'sieu le Professeur?

Of late years I've read very little fiction. But our
former doctor and his wife (Germans--he was a refugee and
she was a Gentile and had to get away from Deutschland
too) persuaded me to read *The Clown* by Heinrich Böll. It
starts off as an anti-Catholic tract in part, but not too bad.

All the best. Write when your time permits. Since my
old friend William McFee died I have had no regular
correspondent of parts except yourself.

Robert

P.S. What do you think of this Mother Seton business?
The universe is too immense for anyone to persist in the
notion of a personal God, I think. A Catholic friend of mine
(Francophile, too) said of the bodily assumption of the
Blessed Virgin that with God all things are possible... Ford
Madox Ford was confessing to an old Passionist priest in a
French village. "Father", he said, "I've tried to be a good
Catholic but I find myself doubting the Immaculate
Conception and the Virgin birth". The old priest regarded
him gravely (Ford was just a lad) and said, "My son, these
are matters for theologians. You be a good boy and believe
all you can."

Dos: Back

Automne au ciel brumeux, aux horizons navrants: Fall with foggy sky, with deceptive horizons.

Mais la mort fuit encore sa grande âme trompée: But death escapes again its great abused soul.

Courage, mon ami, le diable est mort: Cheer up, my friend, the devil is dead.

Paramus, N.J
[non-dated]

Dear Mel,

Your letter was much enjoyed and I should certainly
have replied before this. I know what you mean about the
inquiring students. In my very brief academic career--two
interim appointments to teach novel writing at Columbia
(School of General Studies) there were always unfinished
bits of business after class. I think it's because young
people in spite of all the bravado are uncertain and groping
and value counsel from their elders even though they sneer
at it. And I'm sure you have a lot to say to your charges.
Before I left the Daily News job, I said to a couple of
my colleagues who were going to vote for N---n that my
ethical standards would not permit me to vote for him and
that I considered himself the only real damned scoundrel
who had ever been president of the U.S. Later, I told people
that he and his gang had been preparing a coup. Some of
them agreed, some thought I was seeing things under the
bed. Well, I am glad Dean finally fessed up but he is a
scoundrel nevertheless and the whole lot ought to be in
durance vile--the viler the better. The influence upon the
young of all this reward for evildoing is certainly going to
be bad.
Horrifying to know that Brown U. has put its prices up
to such a towering figure. I could have attended CCNY in
the 20s for about $50 for books and my carfare and lunch
money. Columbia wasn't free but I think $400 would have
been the annual cost.
Worst of all, and saving your presence, most of the
youngsters don't learn anything. Some of the writing and

54

information-lack that I ran into on the newspaper would make your hair curl.

Yes, we all have music as a handicap. My sons are a pianist and violist, my wife plays the violin for fun in the local symphony orchestra, and I, as I believe I've told you, am probably Bergen County's oldest piano pupil. I learn very slowly now and memorize very slowly. Once upon a time--but never mind. It's fun, as you say.

Groucho is often very funny but the hour is late for me--I am in the sack at eleven most nights. For humor I've long been a Benchley and Wodehouse fan. Wodehouse should have had the Nobel Prize--he wrote so beautifully.

We are leaving April 1 for a trip to Charleston, where we'll scrounge lodging from my 84-year-old cousin, eat crab soup and smell the flowers. I shall miss my swimming club.

The enclosed amused us although we are not *Peanuts* addicts. By the way, Maurice Chevalier translated "it was a cinch bet" as "c'était du nougat". The little old lady who turned "Pride's Way" into "Les Voies de l'Orgueil" slopped up on "made him good and tired". She rendered it "le faisait bon et fatigué." Happy Easter!

Robert

C'était du nougat: It was a piece of pie.

Made him good and tired: L'épuisait [in French]

Dear Mel,

I am slow in answering your letter of the 23d ult. Time flies when you are in the sere and yellow.

I have not seem the Cosell show. TV is almost tabu with us except that my severest critic listens to the news broadcasts from 6:30 to 7:30 and we turn on Washington Week in Review every Friday and watch Channel 13 spectaculars--The Duchess of Malfi, Edward the Second, Roberto Devereux. I am sure you are right about Cosell, and shall take your word for it.

We live in a world of things--a lot of them, as you suggest, quite useless. All are designed for prompt replacement, which is cheaper than repairing (if you can get a repairman). Children must have 10-speed bikes--I had an Iver Johnson that cost $30 and it lasted me for years. Our refrigerator dates from 1959 and we drive a 1963 Chevrolet and get almost 25 miles per gal. on the road.

I am not squeamish but Erica Jong sounded like too much for my sensitive male ego. I have read some fairly repulsive books by women, including parts of Xaviera Hollander's lyrical outpourings about her bisexual pleasures, but I don't cultivate them and I don't see blue movies. I respect the privacy even of porno movie stars!

Nowadays, John Ruskin would not be likely to think that his wife's pubic hair was a symptom of disease--which he did.

There was a day when I could read a book a day, or nearly that, and as a reviewer I had to do a lot of fast reading. But now I sit and think, if you call it thinking, a lot more than I read. My wife can read the same novels over and over--Jane Austen, Dickens, Trollope (all right the first time but a whacking bore after that) and even such third-rate stuff as *I, Claudius*. Like you, though, I fairly dote on anthologies and commonplace books and other miscellany. Are you familiar with Curtis and Greenslet's *The Practical Cogitator*? or *The Limits of Art* by Cairns? I have planned a commonplace book of my own but have not got around to assembling it. I also keep after *The Oxford Companion*. Lately I have been reading a few of Cicero's letters in the Loeb Library and struggling (largely in vain) to understand the classic Greek even with a translation. *Dr. Zhivago* was a struggle for me. I have a copy of *Knock* and shall read it. I never got beyond the first couple of volumes of Romain's roman fleuve. You speak of Samuel Eliot Morison. Have you ever read (lighter stuff, true) Stewart Holbrook's various collections about Revolutionary times? I used to like them.

People who sound off about religious doubt are usually bores, but I am glad you more or less agree with me that it's all a cod. I don't object to Christian ethics. My mother-in-law used to say that Christianity seemed like a good thing and that perhaps we ought to try it! Of course she didn't originate that but it expressed her thinking. She was a remarkable person.

Getting back to your observations on the objects by which we are ruled, the local columnist the other day asked if anyone could remember lately having seen a number of things--hoops, pogo sticks, and so on. It was astounding how many children's fads of recent years have vanished. What he didn't ask was when anyone (in our neighborhood at least) had last seen a child with a book. Nobody reads among the blue collar classes and I live in that kind of street. I've questioned some of the youngsters and they say frankly that they "hate" reading. My wife, who began school teaching in the 20s when the new "reading" was coming to the fore, attributes the lack of interest to the long disuse of phonics.

Children can't read new words and the things she and I read as little kids are considered too difficult now. A young lady at the *Daily News* insisted on giving me *Portnoy's Complaint* (also known as *The Gripes of Roth*). I read it politely and asked her didn't people of her age read the Victorians any longer--Hardy, for instance? She said no, they couldn't "relate" to that.

I recently was told that there are about 600 Latin students in the entire New York City high school system. As Dr. Conant said of the B.Sc. degree, "it does not connote a knowledge of science but an ignorance of Latin". Nescire autem quid antequam natus sis acciderit, id est semper esse puerum. No?

I once read all Balzac's fiction--40 volumes--in French. Non sum qualis eram.

Do you enjoy perles ? My favorite is the French schoolboy's translation of Timeo Danaos et dona ferentes: "J'estime les Danois et leur dents de fer."

Time now for my cocktail, table setting, and feeding the cat. More crud in our next. Meanwhile, enjoy your youth and vigor.

Yours ever,
Robert

Roman fleuve: A very lengthy novel with many volumes

Nescire autem quid antequam natus sis acciderit, id est semper esse puerum: You don't know what has happened before you were born, that is to be always a child.

Non sum qualis eram: I am not what I used to be.

Timeo Danaos et dona ferentes: I fear the Greeks even when they bear gifts.

J'estime les Danois et leur dents de fer: I esteem the Danish and their iron teeth.

Paramus, N.J.
October 23, 1975

Dear Mel,

Of course it was pleasant to know that my chatter aroused such enthusiasm. Such notices are rare nowadays for one resting by the wayside.

The long Latin phrase was from Cicero, a man whose works are too little read--by me as well as others. He was a great phrasemaker--old wives' tales, facile precepts, etc. etc. and a great kidder.

My acquaintance with the various perles d'écolier came from a weekly broadcast, French in the Air, which WNYC gets from the Radio Diffusion Française. I don't know where I put the tape recordings, if indeed I made any of these particular schoolboy slips. Boners, we call them. Another that I remember is Il y a trois âges de l'homme-- l'âge de pierre, l'âge de bronze, et l'âge de la retraite.

I am sure you are acquainted with *La dernière chemise de l'amour--Love's Last Shift* (by Congreve?). Victor Hugo, I have learned, was also a rather wild translator--he rendered Frith of Forth le cinquième du quatrième and translated pea jacket paletôt à la purée de pois. Jules Janin translated Macbeth's "Out, out brief candle" as Sortez, chandelle! Perhaps if you wrote under official stationery to the Radio Diffusion Française, mentioned the broadcast, they could tell you where to get a collection of perles. Like you, I love such unconscious humor. A friend of mine, in a book about poisons in our commercial foods, wrote "This attempt at a whitewash boomeranged, leaving the FDA holding a hot potato."

Your parallel quotes from Spiro and Jerry strengthen

my conviction that anyone who votes republican entertains a death wish for his country.

It's very interesting how pornography has come out into the open, so that books you'd have been arrested for owning about 15 years ago are now sold openly. There is a children's book called *Show Me* in which two tots orient each other concerning the various genital and other parts and which, the *Times* review informs us, also showed photographs of fellatio and cunnilingus so that the little ones would, I suppose the idea is, not be shocked if they peered through the keyhole. It reminds me of an old jape about the little fellow who peeked at his parents and remarked, "Gosh! and they spank us for picking our noses!"

Your prediction about Hubert H, is interesting. He does not inspire my confidence exactly, but who does?

Yes, your university is certainly a beautiful creation. If I don't see it before 2000 A.D. I shall certainly not see it, as I shall be just 94, which I by no means expect.

I appreciate your old-fashioned hesitation about using both sides of the paper and admit that I sometimes err that way for the same reason--that I can't find matching paper. This is newsprint I am writing on, the only type of paper I really feel at home with after so many years on a newspaper desk.

I am more or less committed to the University of South Carolina in the matter of memorabilia, Ms., etc. It is possible that I shall be able to obtain a tax saving on my estate (!) by having all the material assessed but I shrink, frankly, from digging it all out.

I have heard too much twaddle from Florence Kennedy's sisters-in-revolt. They are revolting, all right. Dr. Johnson gave the right word on the situation when he said that God had given women so much power that the law had wisely refrained from giving them any more. It is still a seller's market.

Maître Pathelin is a stranger to me. I shall get to it ad kalendas Graecas, most likely. An old friend of mine (almost eighty) wrote to me the other day that he felt rather like a rundown battery. That says it very neatly. By the way, have you ever found out how to pronounce Villon's name as the people of his time pronounced it? One authority as you may recall from an earlier inquiry of mine says it should be Fransway Villion. I was not there.

When I eat ice cream, it has to be a couple of tablespoonfuls as I have spent almost forty years fighting down my appetite. I get too heavy almost after an extra crumb. We used to freeze it ourselves when I was a little chap--frozen peaches was one of the standbys, all cream and fruit... eheu fugaces.

An English or American schoolboy defined the Rialto as "the business end of Venus." There are some howlers of the sort in a little paperback called "The Left-Handed Dictionary."

Right now we are awaiting the news of the death of El Verdugo. He would not have amounted to a hill of beans without Mussolini and Adolf. I shall stick my neck out here and now and state that I do not think Juan Carlos will ever become a titular king, or that if he does he won't stay on the throne long.

Since you are fond of humorous effects, I wonder if you have ever read P. G. Wodehouse? I think that at his best (the things written before the 1940s) he was a great artist. The Oxford Companion once described him as a poet struggling within the confines of farce. His style is impeccable. William McFee complained because W. had not won the Nobel Prize. That, by the way, has gone to what I consider, on small acquaintance, a rather dull poet. Montale is 79. What will he do with that 143 grand?

Pourquoi ne met-on pas d'h devant amour?
(This is an old one)... Parce que l'h mise empêche
l'amour.
I have a long French rebus which I'll copy for you
when I have a bit more energy--my typing gets tough when
I am the least bit tired. I am sitting under an infra-red lamp
trying to suppress my intractable cough, a nuisance.

A bientôt
Robert

Perles d'écolier: A child's blooper

Il y a trois âges de l'homme - l'âge de pierre, l'âge de bronze, et l'âge de la
retraite: There are three human ages - the Stone Age, the Bronze Age and the Retirement
Age.

La dernière chemise de l'amour: The last shirt of love (the last shift of love)

Le cinquième du quatrième: The fifth of the fourth

Paletôt à la purée de pois: Mashed-pea coat

Sortez chandelle: go out, candle!

Ad kalendas Graecas: "to the Greek Kalendae", never ending

Heu fugaces: how swifthly

Pourquoi ne met-on pas d'h devant amour? Parce que l'h mise empêche l'amour:
Why don't we put a "h" before the word "love"? Because the "h" put refrains love.("h
mise": phonetically "la chemise: the shirt)

A bientôt: so long

63

Paramus, N.J.
November 8, 1975

Cher Professeur:

Fremont-Smith really teed off, didn't he? The Times was not any friendlier and told more about some of the details of *Show Me*. You will be pleased to know that the director of the Johnson Library in Hackensack, the central library of Bergan County, took one look at the tome and said "Out!". They had ordered it as a matter of course from St. Martin's Press.

Like you, I oppose censorship and I have no quarrel with anybody's method of pursuing sexual pleasure, odd as some of the means appear to me. But stuffing children with premature knowledge is another thing. No wonder there are so many youthful rapists and so many pregnant girls in high schools. Sex education doesn't make them careful.

À propos de Franglais, I enclose a popular article on argot which may be an old story to you. I have somewhere the classical book in this subject (by Carco, I think) but it's outdated.

I especially liked your sign from the Idaho bar. It's somewhat like the remark the Irishman made when condoling with a friend over the death of the friend's father: "It's what we all come to if we live long enough."

Sorry I am not primed with more perles. You know of course about the French class play in which "left behind" was rendered as "gauche derrière".

My brother once saw a sign in a Greek candy shop on southern N.J.: OUR BEST IS NONE TOO GOOD.

A friend of mine, now departed, loved things like *The*

Unbrownable Mali Sink. I made up one once--about the little foal sired by a great race-horse who thought his whole life would be one of nuzzling his mother and romping around the pasture. He was sold to a race-horse farm, a bitter blow, for he had not realized that in the horse racing game a foal and his mummy are soon parted.

A bird has the biggest brain for its size of any animal. Hence "bird-brain" is not really an effective insult.

El Verdugo is still alive. They must be heating up extra for him in the nether regions. Here, nobody can talk about anything but the coming debâcle in New York City. New Jersey voters turned down four bond issues that would have provided more hospitals, and more work for artisans. It's a mad world, my masters.

I got over-digitalized recently and felt depressed and feeble. I don't know if I ever told you that I have an artificial heart valve (aortic) and rely on several drugs to keep the balance--digitalis, warfarin, and a diuretic plus a potassium supplement.

A favor: Please ask one of your classical colleagues if he knows of a programmed course in classic Greek. I have come to the time of life when concentration is sometimes difficult and I should like to know more of that language before I go to the jardin des refroidis and I get nowhere though I try regularly to rouse myself to a little effort.

The *Times* prints only a tiny percentage of the letters it receives. I don't know what the process of selection is-- they never print anything I send--or I have sent, for I've given up. I used to call attention to their daily illiteracies but what the hell, Archie, what the hell.

The wife of a French ambassador was met at the airport by reporters and asked what she considered the essential thing in life. "Hap-pee-ness", she replied. There was a shocked silence punctuated by giggles and her

husband said, crossly, "Haven't I told you ze word es pronounce: Hop-pee-ness?."
My typing is becoming more and more unreliable tonight so I shall sign off. Ouden pragma, n'est-ce pas?

Keep the words moving,
Robert

À propos de Franglais: about the "French-English" language (a mixture of French and English)

Argot: slang

Gauche derrière:back left

Debâcle: collapse

Jardin des refroidis: garden of dead bodies (cold bodies)

Ouden pragma: and now, the facts

Paramus, N.J.
December 1, 1975

Dear Mel,

I'm glad you like my old jokes! I made up the one about the foal and his mummy. There was something else of the sort in the back of my mind but it has escaped. When it comes back I'll write it down and send it along.

Clémenceau said the same sort of thing about exercise as Mark Twain. He got his exercise going to the funerals of friends who exercised.

Sans doute, je suis une vieille souche--but what is the meaning of souche près d'Athènes? It is a shame that nobody knows a little Latin any more. Dr. Conant said that the B.Sc. degree did not connote a knowledge of science but an ignorance of Latin. You and an ancient friend who is retired and has had a stroke are the only people I know who can take a phrase here and there.

You are right, the junkets do waste the taxpayers money. Participation in government is just a racket for a lot of elected representatives.

I was disgusted by reading in the New York *Times* about Claiborne's $4,000 snack, just as you were. But I am something of a sourpuss about gourmet food and have always believed that wine-tasters were largely frauds. The worst of it was that the food he bought so dear was not very good, in his opinion. His recipes are of course impossible for anyone with a regard for his liver or his cholesterol level--and the time they require for preparation hurts my sense of proportion.

I have been reading a book about Israel's struggle by a Mormon specialist in the Holy Land. All the scheming

67

makes you sick--and there we were helping Nasser just before he turned on us. My younger son's former fiancee was at our house for a few days on her way to Houston from Israel. She is hopeful for Israel but we have other friends who are not. As for the U.N., I think I have responded to your indignation about that business. The building ought to be used as an old folks' home or something of the sort.

I was glad that Butcher Franco had gone to his reward. One wicked scoundrel less! As I said to you, I don't think Carlos will last. I didn't think he would be make king. Nadie es grañde en España hasta que muere.

So your father and I are fellow-cardiacs! I at one time took nitro (not isordyl) but I did not have a coronary at all. The operation (May 1972) took about 5 hours but it saved my life. I had 3 months to live without surgery.

My father died in 1924. Sudden unpredicted heart attack--and our family has drifted apart and scattered-- Texas, Ohio, Long Island, Florida etc. You are luckier. My sons appear to have become confirmed bachelors so I do not expect any grandchildren.

Write your idea about N.Y.C. to the Times. My own solution is to sell it back to the Indians for $16.00.

Have you seen the George Sand series on PR? It's a bit theatrical, I feel.

Thanks.We had an agreeable Thanksgiving. I could not say pertundo tunicamque palliumque in either sense, though, Time takes its toll...

Your cheerfully,
Robert

Je suis une vieille souche: I am an old dolt. (souche also means stump)

Souche près d'Athènes: Dolt near Athens

Nadie es grañde en España hasta que muere: Nobody is great in Spain until he is dead.

Pertundo tunicamque palliumque: I make holes through my tunic and mantle (I work very hard.)

Paramus, N.J.
December 10, 1975

Dear Mel,

I am glad to know another meaning for souche. I did not find the one you meant. Words like that remind me of the Frenchman who abandoned his study of English when he came up against the pronunciation of cough, bough, rough, and sough, and the sign on a theatre marquee reading "cavalcade pronounced success."

I have also learned, via a recording of a Fauré song by Souzay, that there are four syllables in persuader. And when I looked up *Maître Pathelin* upon your mentioning it the fact was borne in upon me that the farce is the source of revenons à nos moutons, which I thought came from Rabelais. So I progress.

Your lofty opinion of my sagesse is appreciated. It has the added value of rarity. We all have our self-doubts. When Fritz Kreisler was interviewed once he said, "When I consider the amount of time I have spent on my feet in drafty halls in strange cities before strangers I do not think too highly of my own intelligence".

Of course it is annoying for anyone to feel that he is not remunerated in a fashion that would show appreciation of what he is and does. It is not the money itself but what it signifies as a reward. However, I have never been on the affluent side--perhaps for a few years when I had a couple of successful books. But this has never really worried me. My wife and I have had some tough going now and then and a few times when the boys were younger it pinched. We have always had simple tastes and we could always get along with a second-hand car--the present one, a little gem, is a 1963 Chevrolet! And our tastes never have run to expensive upholstery or costly clothes. In fact, our only extravagances have been books and music and that on a scale that would not seem high to most people. This is partly owing to my part Alsatian French ancestry. My grandmother and her sisters, with one exception, were the people who held on to dollar bills so tight that they put a permanent wave in George Washington's hair.(Foutre on this portable I am using! too be indolent to bother repairing my other machine.)

What I am getting at is your social equation, if that expresses it. After all you can read and appreciate the world's masterpieces in at least two languages. Can a six-figure income make up for that? And you have the perks that come with your status--the company of kindred souls, access to all of intellectual privileges. You are buying these advantages and the pleasure of working at a profession you cherish (and chose) by accepting a smaller income than Joe Namath. For me there is nothing money can buy that equals leisure and a measure of freedom. And, returning your confidence, my wife and I have about $12,000 a year tax free. We save about one sixth of that every year simply because there is nothing we want that demands large expenditure. As for what you say about the salaries of highschool teachers, no salary is big enough to repay anyone who teaches in the New York high schools. I know some teachers and the tales they tell are horrifying. It is almost as bad out here across the river. Hold fast to that which is good.

My opinion of college graduates of the present day has not been high. Those who came to work for the paper never seemed to know anything. American colleges have degenerated into training schools, and youngsters attend them, not to obtain an education and a source of lifelong pleasure, but in order to get better jobs. A lot of people get into college without even knowing how to read properly and come out hardly better.

As for running over the margins, those same French forebears of mine "crossed" their letters--it's quite legible--to save paper.

The George Sand series is a little ridiculous and pompous, but that 48-year-old gal is tremendous. I could have written a better show, I think.

Louis Simpson, whom I talked once or twice when I was a substitute teacher at Columbia, had a piece in the *Times magazine* Sunday about Delmore Schwartz. If you want to read some perles d'écolier at first hand look up Schwartz's version of *Une Saison en Enfer*. I have marked a few slips in my own copy. Then the thing appeared, I gave it a notice and said I wished the translation had not rendered "troupeaux" as "trumpets." Mary Colum called me up and said she wanted a do a review--she was frothing at the mouth. But we decided that a notice was enough for the work.

Recalling some of the boners you enjoy, I recall from the twenties such gems as "the Rialto is the business end od Venus" and "geometry teaches us to bisex angels". If I can find a copy I'll send you my own deliberate mistranslations of Latin. I do recall sui generis--"They give big portions in Chinese restaurants." I tossed off the thing when Fractured French came out. Unfortunately my publishers had already arranged for a Latin book of the kind.

I once publicly (in a review) scolded a lady who translated Colette's *La Seconde*. She decided that "vous avez bien failli" meant "you completely failed". I forget some of the others.

It is a shame that your work load is being increased. Perhaps things will turn out for the better. Forgive me if I sound like Pangloss now and then. And, by the way, if you can find a volume of Maupassant that contains the story of Dr. Heraclius Glotz, would the U. trust me with it for a day or two? I have a tape I made from a broadcast and there are some words and phrases I just can't hear plainly.

You know, of course, about the American who took a drink of water from a lake in France and then saw the sign "ce lac est bien poissonneux". Or the Englishman who left his friend in their hotel room and told the concierge, as he thought, not to let the fire go out. What he said was "ne laissez pas sortir le fou".

Underlining takes time unless you have an electric. I commend your first resolution and shall take example.

Write when the opportunity offers and you feel like unburdening a peeve or two.

Robert

Revenons à nos moutons: Let's us get back to the point.

Sagesse: wisdom

Sui generis: of its own kind

Perle d'écolier: Schoolboy's blooper

La seconde: The second one

Vous avez bien failli: You almost failed

Ce lac est bien poissoneux: This lake is full of fishes.

Ne laissez pas sortir le fou: Don't let the fool get out.

Paramus, N.J.
December 28, 1975

Dear Mel,

Incredible that it's two weeks since your letter--les jours s'en vont--with your justified remarks about the presidential aspirants and your ominous news about the college budget. Here--I am speaking as a transplanted New Yorker--things are also very bad. Even the Botanical Gardens are pruning (no pun meant) their services. CUNY will charge admission fees and tuition fees!

It was good to hear that your brother had found some encouragement. You just have to keep hacking away until something gives.

You would disown me if you knew how little of that examination I could answer. Made me feel my ignorance keenly. Please send me a copy of the answers.

Tonight will be the last of the George Sand series. I thought it was a little self-conscious, hauling everybody in. We've reserved the Curtis Cate book upon your recommendation.

Recently Public TV showed a French film made during the occupation: *Les Enfants du paradis*. The sound track was bad and as I don't understand spoken French too easily, I was grateful for the English subtitles. The film did not come up to my expectations. I still think *La Kermesse héroïque*, *La Femme du boulanger*, *La Grande Illusion* and the *Marseilles trilogy* the greatest films I have ever seen.

My knowledge of the Maupassant story derives only from the tape I made years ago when WNYC was giving a regular series of readings from French literature. Glotz was a doctor who was really an ape and who massacred all his animal friends, pets and subjects. I believe his name was the title. Some day I'll remember to look things up when I'm in the city, but my usual way is to forget such plans.

So far I have not found my series of Latin translations of which I sent you a sample. I did recall Suum cuique--see my lawyer. And here is a blooper from an America schoolboy: Voici l'Anglais avec son sangfroid habituel-- here comes the Englishman with his habitual bloody cold.

I was also going to say that your exam caught me sans culottes--with my pants down!

Just came up from seeing the last of the Sand series. On the whole I liked it but there was too much loud weeping. And I do not think Flaubert was the one who said that of all the perversions the strangest one is chastity. I was reminded when Chopin breathed his last of what Berlioz said when he heard of C's death--"Il mourait toute sa vie". Read Berlioz' memoirs--he could have been a great writer.

We had a very quiet holiday. My older son came over for dinner and we gave him a few practical gifts. Tomorrow we go down to Toms River to see my convalescent sister in law (2nd hip operation at 79) and Wednesday we are going to a very small New Years' Eve party. There was an insistent fall of snow but not very heavy and the sudden warm change and heavy rain washed it all away.

So much for now. Best wishes for a happy 1976 and quick action by the legislature and governor. Write when the esprit moves.

Yours ever,
Robert

Les jours s'en vont: Days go by

Suum cuique: to each his own

Voici l'Anglais avec son sangfroid habituel: Here is the English man with his habitual composure. (sang-froid in French means both composure and cold blood)

Il mourait toute sa vie: He was dying all his life.

Esprit: Spirit

[After this letter, Robert Molloy no longer underlines every foreign word and/or expression]

Dear Mel,

Thanks for your interesting letter and good wishes.
I have never been in New Orleans, although I have
relatives there (the Barbots) and was talking about them the
day before your letter came. People rave about the place but
I have traveled very little.

You acted beyond the call of friendly duty in
searching out the Gloss story and I am grateful. It is hardly
typical Maupassant and I wonder how it got into Volume
One. I was sure from the tape that the name was Glotz.

From what I have seen of people beyond 80 I do not
wish to exceed that point, as long as I am hanged for rape.
At present I am coming out of a slight slump--post-
operative cough resulting from the opening of my
pericardium in 1973, tendency to wake up constantly
during the night and lose sleep, some breathlessness.
However, I now feel better and as my blood pressure is 130
over 60 a stroke is unlikely!

It is interesting that you do not drink. I never get high
or near it but I have a cocktail by prescription every night
before dinner and a nip before lunch. But I can honestly do
without alcohol. Plain seltzer is my favorite drink.

The Sand series suffered from name-calling or
dropping, Flaubert was just too much. I am sure that
Chopin deathbed business was faked. In the first place, the
Scotswoman gave Chopin, or left for Chopin, a small
fortune which he never got. She was not, to my knowledge,
present in Paris when he was dying. Jane Stirling was her
name. She persuaded him to go to London and Edinburgh,

which put the finale to his TB. The daughter was a little bitch but I am not sure that she destroyed the relationship by interfering with the exchange of mail.

Are you familiar with the poem *Le Manoir de Rosemonde* by Robert de Bonnières? If so, please enlighten me as to the significance of <u>Le Bleu Manoir de Rosemonde</u>... It may be something from a cycle. Duparc set it to music.

In my palmy days as a writer and book reviewer I used to enjoy meeting my confederates and know you had a great time with the Francophiles. I have for years missed the PEN meetings and that sort of thing. My friends now are a few superior newspaper folk, some librarians (through my wife) and some teachers whom I meet at friends' houses but am not on visiting terms with. Everybody lives at some God-awful distance and we more and more dislike driving at night around the metropolitan district.

Today's Times says that in Paris there are several millions of cats, ditto of dogs and huge numbers of goldfish, etc. Yet I don't believe there is a good French word for pet. How come?

1975 is well past, as you suggest. We did have a warm winter. This one is beginning to be nasty, fairly heavy snow today and we were supposed to drive to a concert tonight. My severest critic says NO.

I have still not found my Latin translations but will send you some novelties as soon as my b.w. gets them copied at the library.

Savage attack on George Wallace by a Southerner in today's *Times magazine*. They are usually more objective. I am sorry for Nixon and Wallace, much as I detest both. Their inner life must be dreadful.

So much for the nonce. All the best for '76. Aequam memento...

Cura ut valeas,
Robert

Aequam memento: Remember to be fair.
Cura ut valeas: Take care of yourself.

Paramus, N.J.
January 29 1976,

Dear Mel,

Rien de nouveau. We've had snow and rain, biting cold and mildness, and I appear to have got over the fit of physical depression (a syndrome composed of shortness of breath, a static cough and interrupted sleep.)

I used to talk at academic tauroboliums and women's clubs--had a contract at one time but hated the travel part. I could give a reading in Gullah! I know of one local raconteur who was introduced as a great story teller to a group of elderly females and he was embarrassed at not being able to remember one single clean joke.

My last photo led to suit by the photographer for damage to his camera! But I'll get someone to make a good snapshot. Usually my pictures are the sort of things that cause miscarriages.

Happy to hear about the demoiselle from Philadelphia. I have been married so long that we are into our second bottle of Tabasco sauce (47 years this June). I wish my sons would get wives for themselves.

Disgusting about the Concorde. We are going to be choked to death sooner or later--perhaps I shall not live to experience it.

Early rising is one of the secrets of success (take it from a failure who knows them all).

So far I haven't latched on to the *Weight Watchers* magazine but will. I am glad your brother and his collab. have made a start. Breaking the ice can be tough.

I told you that this god old Royal typewriter had jammed. I could not face taking it to a store--they would have told me that something or other was "shot" and charged more than it is worth. Tonight I just happened to touch the keys and lo and behold the jam had disappeared. Magic, that's what.

I envy your energy. I tire easily and the M.D. says "What do you expect?," when I complain about it. The Jules Verne job should be very interesting indeed. I used to love *20,000 Lieues sous la Mer* and *The Mysterious Island*.

The enclosed are Morris Bishop's version of songs that were popular when I was a boy and youth. If they are not familiar to you ask your father. Of course I don't mean Frankie and Johnny or Auld Lang Syne! I've always enjoyed this sort of thing. I suppose you know Francis Steegmuller's versions of *The Owl and the Pussycat*, etc.?

I've recalled some more of my Liberated Latin:

> Troja fuit (let's dance)
> Modus operandi (a fashionable operation)
> Suum cuique (call my lawyer)

and in French :

> Tour de Force (a police parade)

I look forward to your discoveries about *Manoir de Rosemonde*. You are like me in not letting such things drop.

It's always good to hear from you. My other friends, when they write at all write notes of two or three sentences.

Remember the epigram from *Les Enfants du paradis*--"L'amour est simple".

My wife is re-reading Proust (in English). I have heard that there is a new translation in the works. Do you know about it? I do not wish to re-read that unhappy long work--the people in it, with notable exceptions, would have made good staff members in Nixon's White House. The parts about the Verdurins are not too bad, though, or the part about his childhood. A painter friend of mine once said that the parts about Elstir were pure nonsense. And was Bergotte Anatole France? Speaking of that, do you know about the librettists who were turning Thaïs into an opera? They called Paphnuce Athanaël because there were only two French words that rhymed with Paphnuce--puce and prépuce. Forgive me if I've repeated that...

I look forward to the Maupassant you so kindly sought out for me. That's all for the nonce.

Mes salutations les plus empressées

R. M.

Rien de nouveau: Nothing new

Raconteur: Storyteller

Demoiselle: Young lady

Troja fuit: Troy has been

Modus operandi: Mode of operating

Suum cuique: to each his own

Tour de force: feat of strength

Mes salutations les plus empressées: my best regards

Dear Mel,

As I have apparently misplaced your last letter (sangdieu--just found it)--I was going to say that this might be a little more scatterbrained than usual. I have been reading Strachey's youthful essays--prodigious for a man between 25 and 30--and he devoted a long piece or series to the English letter writers. You are right, it is a lost art, and a lost pleasure. I don't suppose most youngsters write letters at all.

The interview was a very happy one, not gushing. So far I haven't come up with a *W.W.* magazine but will write to the fountainhead for a copy. Good luck to your brother and his collaborator.

Once, long ago, I thought I might set out to be an 18th century authority but you know what happens to the best-laid schemes... Not so long ago I resumed with a biography of Jefferson, but the author sight of a lot of his problems. Now that the Adams Chronicle is (are?) in full swing (and what do you think of it? (them?), I have been considering the first years of the U.S. but keeping it secret lest they think I am taking part in this disgusting overemphasis of the Bicentennial. Those early democrats (or republicans, really) were amazing men and it would be most interesting to trace in detail their response to Locke, the Encyclopedie and such people as your Montesquieu.

I have never had the dubious pleasure of meeting la capote américaine (these americans, what sentiment!) and although I read his first youthful book I have never been tempted to try again. Truman Capote is just a little too feminine, even for a homosexual (and I am not intolerant). I'd take issue with you on male vanity, though. Young men today are peacocks, although the new styles are so inharmonious and ill-shaped. I do think, however, that Truman is dedicated to his profession and that he writes with simple elegance.

Kunstler once reviewed a book of mine very favorably, so I have been making allowances for him! But I think he has gone over the edge now. Quos vult deus perdere... Isn't it strange that most of the politicians who are assassinated are well-intentioned men? I except Wallace and his like. They shot at Harry Truman and Roosevelt but apparently nobody thought our recent luminary worth the risk.

I envy Maurice Goudeket, Colette's last husband. Right now I am getting over a slight cold--first in three years--and I feel that the golden years are a little tarnished. Have I told you that at Père Lachaise we saw a typical middle-aged schoolmarm leading her little ones (really young children) to Colette's tomb and telling them enthusiastically about her. Autre temps, autres moeurs. Nowadays, though, Colette must seem tame to the young. A digression--this typing is the result of my cold hangover and not because I am losing my tactile skill... Oddly enough, I had been in much better shape before the cold came on; I had been gaining too much weight and getting short-winded and finally my doctor saw the light and ordered a chest x-ray. As I myself knew, there was congestion. An addition to my diuretic regime did the trick - lost ten pounds in about a week and felt immensely benefited. Doctors must be goaded sometimes.

My severest critic, Marion, has just re-read the Painter books but has not come across the Sheppard--Shattuck, I mean. She is a compulsive reader, which I am not. I am glad that I read P. when I was younger (began it at 22, read half in French) but I don't think I shall go through it again unless someone makes an abridgement. I shall try my s.c. on the questions. Moncrieff made a fine translation of a pun: Mme. Verdurin, --it was Mme de Guermantès,--said of Charlus that he was "Taquin le Superbe", alluding, as you remember, to his teasing somebody or other about a piece of property. Moncrieff rendered it "Teaser Augustus."

We had a terrific storm also, but no damage here. Our present house, thank God, has no cellar.

The Concorde, this monster flying machine, should not be permitted to foul up our already polluted atmosphere. A friend of mine, years ago, had to sell his Long Island house when the jets began to land and take off at Kennedy.

Charleston, apparently, had a good time over the diapers for the chevaux. In my day old ladies interested in their gardens used to fight for the piles of crottin heaped up by the street sweeper.

Thanks for telling me about the re-translation of the last part of Proust. Moncrieff, too, has had his critics.

I dredged up from memory another couple of daffynitions: My brother I believe, originated one, about "cul de sac" meaning "air the mattress". My own is carpe diem (Friday).

Tell me your conclusions on the Hearst affair, please. Any glimmer of info. about *Le Manoir de Rosemonde*? And what was Maupassant's first published story, which Flaubert, after coaching him for so long, pronounced a masterpiece? I have lost track of the story.

Give me the continued pleasure of your correspondence when you are able to spare some time from what appears like an appallingly busy life.

Robert

My wife has just returned from luncheon with my sister-in-law and two ladies, both 99 years old. One is from Charleston. I knew her sons.

Sang-dieu: My goodness

Quos vult deus perdere: Those whom God chooses to condemn

Autres temps autres moeurs: Other times, others customs

Carpe diem: Make the road of the day.

Paramus,N.J.
March 9, 1976

Dear Mel,

Thank you very much for the Tillier book and the warm inscription. I have read half and shall terminate the reading tonight. I think you have made a strong case for Tillier and that you certainly have produced a thoroughly professional piece of work. Keep it up--how about Loti as a subject? I'll comment further when I am thoroughly myself. The last two weeks have been rather a mauvais quart d'heure--the cold I mentioned was succeeded by very bad nosebleeds, necessitating two visits to a hospital emergency ward, the injection of Vitamin K and withdrawing of my anti-coagulant, not without some risk as you know. I was also forbidden coffee or tea and alcoholic drinks. Everything is fortunately clearing up now and I shall resume swimming tomorrow and go on with my piano and vocal lessons. Dabit Deus his quoque finem.

The Girtha strip seems to me to have made a fine start. Remind your brother (if he won't mind) that the field of reducing plans of the crank and crash variety also offers a great deal of room for ridicule. I hope some syndicate will pick up the strip.

I have looked through the college paper in which you wrapped the Tillier opus. I do not doubt that yours students write better French than their colleagues' English! I enclose a clipping pointing to the same situation. The *Times* had another article which got away from me about the teachers of English in colleges who have complained that their freshman students cannot write a simple correct sentence. I suspect that a lot of the high school teachers cannot either.

The Cate biography certainly gives the lie to the TV series, which I thought was at least true to fact. Cate has done a fine job of research and recreation. As a retired copy editor, I cannot help the feeling that he deserved better editing and even proof reading but nobody cares nowadays. I particularly deplore the somewhat obsessive sentence structure and I was taken aback by the mistranslation of a line from Metastasio and the fact that Mr. Cate has the Immaculate Conception and the Virgin Birth confused in his mind--as for that matter do many people. But these are minor. I am enjoying the leisurely narrative.

I do not think I told you that we have adopted another cat. Our regular cat is a neutered female picked up from the street--a beautiful fawn-colored Abyssinian type with a white belly and legs, whom we named Fulvia. The new arrival is a young Tom, orange colored with white, not as beautiful but very charming. He was hanging around the Boys Club where we swim and I took him home. We saw to his shots and now he must have his cosmic viewpoint altered three weeks from now (he is not quite 8 months old). We have named him Mark Antony although I do not know if we can exactly refer to him as Fulvia's mate! They romp very roughly at present--you would think they were out to kill but it is just noise and high spirits, although, being still a kitten, he wants to play more than Fulvia, who is five years old. A cat is the perfect pet for older folk, clean as a pin, careful of bric-à-brac and not in need of outdoor exercise.

I have been reading Barbara Brown's *New Minds, New Bodies*, which is about biofeedback, which may be the answer (I don't profess to know!) to the psychomatic medicine problem. I myself have used hypnosis with good results. A psychologist cured my younger son of stage fright by means of hypnotic suggestion and he immediately played an audition and was hired for the Houston Symphony, in which he still plays.

Also an interesting book is Birmingham's *The Grandees*, about the Sephardic Jews in the U.S. Most people know little about them and do not even recognize their names as those of Jewish families. My mother's cousin married a S.J. named Ashley Tobias--he had lots of money, drove a Cadillac down the main avenue every morning. We were not very intimate--don't mean unfriendly, but the Sephardim are very haughty folk. Uriah Levy was one of them and so was the Confederate Secretary of War, Judah Benjamin. They despised the German Jews who came here in the 1840s and were the subject of another book by Birmingham, *Our Crowd*. Both despised, by the way, the Polish and Russian Jews who came last of all. It's always possible to look down on somebody. There were a lot of partly Latin Jews in Charleston--with such names as Montague, Triest, Ottolengui--I think the last were French.

There are making a great fuss over the film of *Barry Lindon*. It is not in my set of Thackeray but I shall buy the paperback that has come out. Are you familiar with the novel? Thackeray is often hard going--he was a good enough writer but to my mind a bad technician, putting all the "scenes" into narrative and making "scenes" of little importance. Just backward. He was only 36 when he wrote *Vanity Fair*. If he had been able to wait until he had read *Madame Bovary* he might have done better. As a matter of fact, he disliked it, considering it a heartless picture of a woman's degeneration.

Speaking of narrative technique, I am plagued by a friend, 56, my former straw boss at the News, who wants to write a novel. He is not a fool by any means but it has been a major exercise in tact to persuade him that he must acquire some fictional technique, of which, although he is well read and perceptive, he hasn't the faintest notion. Some people want to begin at the top. I spent years studying the writing of fiction - two of them at N.Y.U. I wrote a story <u>every week</u> and finally the instructor (a good friend of mine but merciless) handed back one with the words, "A very professional piece of work." It was my big moment. I sold that and a companion story later and the two of them were the basis of my starting out on *Pride's Way*. As my old boss at the Sun used to say of his earlier efforts, "I was a genius then."

Again many thanks for the book. It will go among my autographed volumes, side by side with William McFee, Benêt, Robert Frost, etc... As Emerson said to Whitman, I salute you at the beginning of a great career.

All the best,
R. M.

Mauvais quart d'heure: To have a bad time (for 15 minutes)

Dabit Deus his quoque finem: God will put an end to these (troubles).

Paramus, N.J
[postcard, no date]

Stop Press...

The Maupassant book arrived today while our car was laid up by snowpiles. Hence this insert. Beautiful edition-- they must have it rebound.

I have been enjoying the story a lot. The tape I have was cut heavily, took much of the point out.

Many thanks. More later and a report on Tillier. Hackensack Library gets all the Twayne series.

Robert

Paramus, N.J.
March 21, 1976

Dear Mel,

Hymen o Hymenaee! Felicitations. Be sure to bring Miss Cindy to see us. I wish my sons would take wives unto themselves. I know you'll be very happy, aided not a little by a community of interest. I recall your telling me that you met at a convention.

I much enjoyed your book on Claude Tillier. I wonder how many readers will grasp the significance of Dr. Minxit's name? How will you treat Jules Verne if you be a biog? I don't think there's much "literary" value in his works--or is there?

By now I hope you have received the Maupassant, which I returned a few days ago. The Dr. Gloss story has much more meaning in a full version--the tape was butchered--but I do not think it is top-drawer Maupassant. As it was not published until ten years after his death he must have judged it unfavorably. Nevertheless it was interesting and often amusing. I took the opportunity of re-reading *Boule de Suif*, certainly a masterpiece (I feel a little doubtful about the final scene, unlovable as the people were.) Many thanks for your kind labor in tracking down the volume for me.

I'll send the copy of *The Reunion* in tomorrow's mail. No, I have not re-read it. The notices were varied--a couple of small town reviewers said it was a soap opera. I do recall that it was the first ms. I gave to my then new agent, Paul Reynolds. I had rewritten a novel for one of his clients but he did not know my original work. He called me one afternoon at the newspaper where I was working and said.

"This is pretty impressive stuff. A man who could write this and bothers to rewrite other people's stuff ought to have his head examined." That was nice, anyway.

I just went downstairs to close the garage door--a real spring squall had sprung up. Our forsythia is open and we've had a lot of crocus. I tried spading a bit of the veg. garden this morning to see how the ground was doing and it seems ready for planting.

I have decided not to renew our yearly membership in MENSA. It was pleasant to know that we were smart enough to be admitted but actual membership is not profitable, as we do not go to their meetings and are not interested in bridge, ESP, or backgammon--not the sort of things that ought to occupy the upper 2 per-centile of the population! I wonder if you are a member?

I recalled another schoolboy perle--a British boy translated Le peuple ému répondit as "the purple emu laid another egg."

Was the Molière modernized? I have a recording I must play again.

My salutations to Miss Cindy. Explain to her that I am a copain de plume (my translation!). Most affectionately,

Robert

Hymen o Hymenaee! /Felicitations: Felicitations for a wedding (congratulations).

Le peuple ému répondit: The people, (who were) moved, answered.

Copain de plume: Pen pal

Dear Mel,

Thank you for the collection of perles. I shall show them this weekend to my friend Morris Schreier, who teaches French in a public high school.

Since you are interested in word play and the like, I suggest that you look at *Words at Play* by Willard R. Espy. It can be had in a rather costly paperback, otherwise the university library is I suppose the best resource. I am also planning to copy some French limericks, the work of George DuMaurier, for you.

I'm not sure I told you that I had finished the Sand biog. It was a fine research job and skillfully executed but I wish I had been asked to read copy on it. Copy editing, and proof reading, have both gone to hell in a published world of rising costs. I was a bit annoyed by references to Liszt's "transpositions" for piano when the word was "transcriptions". One of the Chopin impromptus was listed in the wrong key. There were dozens and dozens of such flyspecks. But a darned good book.

Prodded by the Adams Chronicles, I am re-reading with much pleasure *The Education of Henry Adams*. If you have not read it be sure to do so.

A young fiancé is a busy man--but were you able to find out anything about *Le Manoir de Rosemonde* and its author Robert de Bonnières?

We are having a burst of nice weather today--it has been too windy most of the time in spite of clear skies. We hope you'll have nice holiday weather with Miss Cindy.

Little by little I am recalling more and more of the

liberated Latin I invented. Another is <u>pro bono publico</u>--a Potter's field. I was a genius in those days, as my old boss used to say.

I was reminding my beautiful wife of the sick joke attributed to a Frenchman when, attending a Bernhardt performance, he remarked, when the trois coups sounded, "Voici Sarah". I put the accent on the second syllable of <u>Sarah</u>. My b.w. thought this was wrong. Please advise.

What comments have you had on the Tillier? There is always someone who knows better, as I can tell you from long and sometimes annoying experience.

Write when you can disengage your thoughts from the really important aspect of life as dictated by your present happy situation!

Your ever,
Robert

Pro bono publico: For the good of the state

Trois coups: Three knocks which indicate, in the theater, that the play is about to begin.

Paramus, N.J.
April 29, 1976

Dear Mel,

It was good to know that the nuptials are set. Trust there will not be too many duplications of fish slices--that was what the Wodehouse characters always thought of sending. Nine days after your wedding will be our 47th anniversary. Don't be in any hurry to catch up.

I must have sounded pushy about the Bonnières info. When I'm in New York I'll try my luck at the NYPL. You are the only French scholar I know.

The sickness of the joke about Sarah Bernhardt was that the fellow who said "voici Sarah" was alluding to her wooden leg stomping across the stage. When my father was head auditor at the shipping board offices in Philadelphia (1917-18), he took a personable young man away from his job as bellhop at the Ritz-Carlton(?) in Phila. and turned him into a clerical worker. That was the hotel at which Sarah put up in that city, and McCartney used to make us laugh (unfeelingly) with his account of how he pushed her up the stairs.

We've had all sorts of weather here too 25º one day, killed all the magnolia blossoms overnight; then 96º about a week late. But now the dogwoods and azaleas and the young green leaves are inimitable. I never saw them so lush.

Thanks for the beautiful André Chénier poem. I blush to admit that I had to look up Palès. As for the poet's plaidoyer, I am ignorant. Did he claim to be an orphan? Ironic that if Robespierre had died two days sooner Chénier would have been freed. I do not know why a Stoic should be mentioned except to heighten the classical atmosphère.

Mr. Humphrey put it on the line today. I still think he is the only hope. I will not vote for a man who uses his nickname officially (snob, n'est-ce pas?) and I shall never under any circumstances vote for a Republican presidential candidate. So I may default. If you care to look up the record, in 120 years the Republicans have given us fourteen presidents, only two worth a damn--T.R. and Lincoln. The Democrats have elected only six and every one of them was first-rate. My theory is that this country has a death wish. I believe the Hackensack library has a standing order for the Twayne series but I'll prod them.

Hic jacet (a sport coat.)

My best to you and mes amitiés à Mlle Cindy.

R. M.

Palès: Goddess who protected the animals

Hic jacet: Here he lies

Mes amitiés: My kind regards

Paramus, N.J.
May 24, 1976

Dear Mel,

I enjoyed reading the French exams but must plead nolo contendere on your offer to correct my answers. I am hopelessly behind on everything but the conventional literature and my prose would give too many soufflets to Vaugelas! I write French the way most Frenchmen speak English. Strictly sens unique with me.

Life is uneventful here except for gardening and the depredations of our younger cat. Today he broke through the window screen and "escaped". I have been reading some books about Chartres (the Adams Chronicles started me off on Henry) and other French cathedrals and feel a strong urge to have another look at la belle France. But my helpmeet travels rather poorly--water, foods etc., and the chances of our going are remote.

About the Melville "total immersion": I am a bit of a Philistine about these matters and though I know the idea is a worthy one it has a ritual quality--like piling up indulgences through numerous pious practices. There is too much cetology in Melville to begin with, and experienced readers usually skip it. Melville himself was taken aback by the various symbolic interpretations of his work. He said he knew there was something of a parable quality in it but did not go beyond that. His *Omoo* and *Typee* are more readable than *Moby Dick*. Stevenson said Melville "had no ear." What do you think? Am I just a crusty senescent? Does imaginative literature demand or justify so much exegesis?

98

<u>Hic jacet</u>: a sports coat. Or do I repeat?

I also enjoyed the joke about the honeymooners. I trust he "showed his manhood" and "asserted his independence" right on the spot.

All good wishes, mon cher, and mes amitiés à Mlle Cindy.

Robert

Sens unique: One way

Paramus, N.J.
June 17, 1976

Dear Mel,

There isn't much news down this away so I haven't been writing much to anyone. The heat has been excessive, spoiling the end of spring. Our car's air conditioner conked out just the day before we were to drive down to the shore to see my aged brother and sister-in-law. It wasn't too bad on the highway but we dreaded getting stuck in heavy traffic.

An old (79) newspaper colleague writes from Florida that the latest bicentennial observance is that of a local prostitute, who in honor of the occasion has lowered her price to her price to $17.76 but will take only minute men.

We are distressed about Carter--do not feel warmed toward him and dislike the idea of a president with a nickname, officially that is. What kind of image will we have with the rest of the world with a chief exec. named Jimmy? Of course it would be impossible to vote for Ford. I think I shall write in for Humphrey if Carter is the candidate, as seems inevitable.

I note that your noces are right around the corner and wish you and Miss Cindy all kinds of happiness and good fortune. The day before your wedding will be the fiftieth anniversary of the first trip my wife and I made to the beach together, in 1926. It was a murky day but she was painfully sunburned. Our 47th anniversary is coming up. Don't quote me, but time flies.

Going through my papers to get my desk in order, a losing task, I found a contrived ending that I contrived years ago. This jape goes as follows: A man standing in a

100

subway train was irritated when a hoodlum sitting right beneath him lighted a cigarette. "God damn you, put that out!" he shouted, whereupon the hood pulled out a pistol and shot him dead. This was stander's last cuss. (I was a genius then, as my old boss used to say).

Incidental literary note: It is not generally known nowadays that Cicero was a great phrasemaker. He invented facile princeps, old wives' tales, strain every nerve, and the breeze of public favor. He was also, as I suppose you know, a great wit. Somebody put out a collection of his gags, many years ago, and I had a look at it once in the public library but it disappeared.

I think I told you that we now have two cats, Fulvia (because she is tawny) and, a ginger and white cat, Mark Antony, since he was F's husband. Mark A. is also neutered but very masculine at ten months old. Fulvia is very feminine despite the surgery. Hormones are not everything, apparently.

I have taken up Loren Eiseley. Do you know his work?

That's all for now. All best wishes and we hope to meet you and your bride before too many moons have waned.

Robert

Noces: Weddings

Facile princeps: Easily first

Paramus, N.J.
July 22, 1976

Dear Mel,

It was good to have your letter. I had not written while you still presumably were on your honeymoon.

I don't envy you the job of moving. We came here to our Cape Cod doll house none years ago from a cellar--two stories-and-attic-house easily twice as big--and getting rid of unneeded furniture and extra books, plus the resettling, was a tough chore all around.

I am still not enthusiastic about "Jimmy"--a cheap nickname for a president, as perhaps you've already read in my opinionated correspondence. But I took a solemn oath several years ago never to vote for any Republican again, and Ford is a terrible chump as well as the man who, in Anthony Lewis' phrase, granted "a shameless pardon to a shameless man." I wanted Humphrey to try but I am sure he made a wise decision. Have I written to you that in 120 years the GOP has elected fourteen presidents, only two of whom were worth a damn, whereas the 7 Democrats have all had a good deal of merit, though of course none was faultless.

Our 47th milestone was passed on June 29. My wife-to-be was sunburned at Brighton Beach June 19, 1926.

I don't know if any good will be done by reopening the question of who killed Zipper Jack. Maybe some jealous husband or lover had something to do with it.

William A. Rusher is a bit too much to the right to suit me, but he couldn't be far wrong about porno. I have never seen one of the blue pictures that are so popular now, not because I'm squeamish but because I don't consider sexual intercourse a fit subject for graphic presentation of the kind it's getting. Yes, please send me the clipping if you can dig it up.

Capote is an old woman. I suspect he is either eunuchoid or homosexual and the stuff he writes does not interest me. Speaking of writing, I have read for the first time the first two volumes of *The Tales of Genji*--enough for the time being. A strange civilization, that of 11th century Japan! Are you familiar with the work? Different from the Japan Pierre Loti wrote about in *Madame Chrysanthème*.

I have little to report. It's been a bad late spring and early summer here.

The enclosed clipping is amusing but as usual it has a typical N.Y *Times* gaffe. Nobody looks up anything.

My salutations les plus empressées to Madame--and yourself.

R. M.

Salutations les plus empressées: With my best regards

Paramus, N.J.
August 9, 1976

Dear Mel,

I am glad you approve of my ten-cent philosophy. As for running for president, I'd rather be right.

Some wit has said that if Carter had figured in the cherry tree story he would have said, "Well, Father--yes and no." But the alternative is so dismaying that I shall take a chance on him. By doing so I hope to put a final nail in the coffin of the GOP. Eric Sevareid said tonight, according to my wife (I never listen to the news broadcasts on TV because the ads disgust me) that there is going to be a bloody battle at Kansas City and that it may very well bring the breakup of the Republican Party.

It is storming here, mostly rain, however, at 9:30 p.m. I trust you will have escaped the effects of the hurricane.

I am glad that l'amour est vainqueur de tout with you. I should feel lost without my moitié!

The trip to Paris fills me with envy. I loved the city although I spent only a week there. I have a record of Colette reading from *Chéri* and the novel about the little girl being trained to be a high-class prostitute. I share her love for cats. Our younger one, Mark Antony, went off his feed for three days and my wife and I were terribly distressed. But he got over it. The vet couldn't find a thing wrong. (It occurs to me that when you receive this letter you will have returned from France...).

We enjoyed the fable. Could you say c'est la merde qui nous console, hélas, et qui nous fait vivre?

I have never read anything by old Agatha Christie. Whodunits are not in my list of pleasures, I am sorry to say.

I loved *The Moonstone*, though. My wife reads one every week but she does not care for Christie. I like some of Faulkner's short stories and I was fond of that grisly thing, *Sanctuary*, and admired *Intruder in the Dust*. Some of my literary friends used to put *The Sound and the Fury* at the top of the list. I was rather cool to it. I think more and more that literature should cultivate the élite--there's been too much about the stupid and inarticulate, not to say the neurotic which is the contemporary trend. I liked Steinbeck's *The Grapes of Wrath* and *Of Mice and Men*. By the way, did you know that somebody called *Portnoy's Complaint* "*The Gripes of Roth*?"

Reagan would do anything to get the nomination. And Richard Schweicker, like the prime minister in *The Prisoner of Zenda*, apparently has two speeches in his pocket.

I should say that Mrs. Yoken's scrabble move proves that she is a witch (in a complimentary sense, naturally).

Thanks for your kind invitation. We'll get together yet. The cats are a bit of a problem--no neighbors we can trust to see after them so we have to kennel them.

Yours ever,
R. M.

L'amour est vainqueur de tout: Love conquers all.

My "moitié": My half (my wife)

C'est la merde qui nous console, hélas, et qui nous fait vivre.: That's excrement which comforts us, alas, and makes us live.

Dear Mel,

Responding to your flattering estimate of my lucubrations, I put myself in the position of Montaigne and Socrates and will do the best I can.

First of all, I share your disgust with the political convention system and the brainless way we choose our representation. But what can be done about it? Ford buys the presidency with what Anthony Lewis called "a shameless pardon for a shameless man." Ford, not giving a damn about the capabilities of his successor (if Dole should be such) selects a political picador to torment Carter and thus further Ford's desire to be selected. I did not care for Baker on the strength of his Watergate showing but Ford could have done a whole lot better than Dole--who has been caught with his pants down over a campaign contribution from the anti-abortionists. He's also get to explain the I.T.T. affair. I think Carter and Mondale will give him a fairly tough tussle. Ford, in my estimation, is a bigger chump than Eisenhower. Reagan, of course is a cheapjack and ought to be fairly invisible for a while. The Richard Schweiker choice was the biggest floater imaginable.

So I'm still backing Carter, religion and all notwithstanding. Politics is the art of the possible, as some pundit remarked, and I'd have preferred McCarthy but what's done is done.

Obviously your bride is a formidable Scrabbler. When we took the test for MENSA membership years ago, my b.w. got a higher rating than I did but she wears her superiority agreeably. I told her that if she had been admitted and I had not I would divorce her a mensa et thoro! Do not be surprised at anything a smart woman can do.

I think the Bantam dictionary fellow showed a bit of sporting blood at that. The show had to go on and the dict. had to be put out at a certain time. It would make it look terribly out of date not to have a 39th president named. After all, a number of papers reported Dewey's election in 1948 and survived with just a bit of ridicule. I have a hunch that Carter will finish ahead. We shall see.

I have not seen any serpents in our neighborhood so far. Snakes, as you know, come downhill when there is a drought. I think the drought may be over now. We've had a couple of rainstorms and others are predicted.

I am concerned about all this fooling around with man-made genes. Something like the events in Wells' *The Food of the Gods* could happen.

I have been replaying my Pathé recording of *Cyrano* (with the younger Coquelin) and I am happy to say that I can still respond to it, no matter what the academicians say. I still choke over the last act of Bohême, too, and Violetta's final aria. Underneath my forbidding exterior an old softly is hidden, I'm afraid. What do you think of the above-mentioned chestnuts?

I envy you your girl bride and your numerous friends. We live in a largely blue-collar neighborhood and most of my contemporaries are either distant or dead. We used to give musical parties when my sons were both at home and we had a bigger house--quintets, trios, quartets, piano solos--on and on. William McFee was my last faithful correspondent before you. Keep the letters coming when you have a few moments to spare.

I saw Paris for only a week but I loved every minute

of that time. To shuttle between London and Paris would be the most wonderful privilege--add an occasional trip to Florence and the vicinity of Nîmes and Arles. We spent a week in Uzès (Gard) in an inn with fifteenth century walls and fourteenth century plumbing and a hostess with a slim figure, classical features* and violet eyes (I think l'hôtesse was Turkish). Eheu fugaces. She used to chuckle (I don't know at what) when I said to her that at breakfast we liked to sit in the coin tiède. (The place, as Benchley said of a New England bedroom in midwinter, had the temperature of a well-regulated crypt).

Well, voilà tout for the nonce. My cats are demanding their late evening snack.

I have just re-read Allen's *Only Yesterday*. Get it if you haven't read it. I'm not reading the sequel, *Since Yesterday* . I was the man,I suffered, I was there...

We send our congratulations on your happiness. Please convey them to Mrs. Y.

Yours ever,
Robert

We sold our 1963 Chevrolet (still a fine little heap but cranky) and got a new Toyota. The prices of cars are frightful!

* I think l'hôtesse was Turkish. Mm-mm!

A mensa et thoro: From the table and the marital bed

Eheu fugaces: How swiftly

Coin tiède: Comfortable nook

Voilà tout: That's it.

Paramus, N.J.
September 26, 1976

Dear Mel,

Were you greatly impressed by the debate? I thought it was fairly dull. Shannon said in today's *Times* that the choice was between a possible second Roosevelt and a second Coolidge; that Ford would do nothing but coast along playing golf weekends.

We had a respectable but uninteresting ten days at the shore. I cannot swim in surf--too much sudden effort necessary--but we bathed, walked, ate some rather poor restaurant dinners. My better half is an excellent cook and came home gladly. Great satisfaction of the trip was our little Toyota which we have had just a month. It's a great little car.

Friday I go for my regular proctoscopy. The worst thing about that is the dose of castor oil the night before. I dread it. My rear admiral uses a Japanese device, a flexible tube with a camera, a pair of scissors and an electrical doodad that cauterizes the polyps that are sniped off. This, however, is just for inspection. A nuisance but que voulez-vous?

Today it has rained rather steadily, just holding up about five-thirty. My wife and I got the iris dug up, separated, and replanted. We have some chrysanthemums just starting to bloom. The cosmos are still going strong and the marigolds have finally come across--Burpee's Seeds Grow Slowly, if you ask me. We have lettuce and a few tomatoes (bad season for them) and a zucchini or two. But the fall is drawing on. Automne aux horizons navrants ...

I have pulled myself together in the attempt to carry out my project of re-writing *The Bride of Lammermoor* but the local libraries are not helpful on the historical background of Scott's novels and two history books have failed to pin down the time, which I have to know.

Scott dictated the novel from his bed of pain and although the story is a great one and the book is almost my very favorite the style and construction are hard for modern readers. I'm going to get the job done, but it's just for fun. I may send you the m.s. if I'm satisfied with the job I do.

Tuesday I resume voice lessons with my pretty young teacher. The results are not such as to send scouts out to hear me but I get some fun out of the process. Odd thing is that with age my range has risen slightly and the quality has changed from bass to baritone.

But not high enough to sing the Prologue to Pagliacci! At seventy I must sound a bit foolish singing love songs. A propos de chant, they have put out a Caruso record reconstituted by means of a computer, reconstructing the performance. The difference is quite noticeable.

I learned just recently that crapaudalso means grand piano (slang).

Are you and Miss Cindy fairly well settled in after all the moving? And what about the new semester?

This portable is breaking my back and spirit. My old apparatus has got stuck. So I'll sigh off here. Just one more thing--we saw *All the President's Men*, a damn good picture. Probably you have already seen it.

All the best,
R. M.

Que voulez-vous: What can you say?

Automne aux horizons navrants: Fall with its deceptive horizons

A propos de chant: About song

Paramus, N.J.
11 October, 1976

Dear Mel,

Thank you for the jeu d'esprit. It made me look up trémas, and guillemets too. Pourquoi ne met-on pas d'hache devant "amour"?

I share your disgust with the powers that be--in your case the sovereign state of Massachusetts. There's always money for bombers, missiles, new sports stadiums (stadia if you like) and so on but the New York Public Library--truly a noble institution--is open just half the hours it used to be open. Figure that. It is chiefly private, not public, and the city has no money for it, apparently. Yet lots of us owe what education we have to the N.Y. Public Library system.

I have been calling Ford a stumblebum and now he has really gone and torn it. The fact that he could have been caught so far off base on the Eastern Europe situation doesn't suggest that he knows much of what's going on in the world, does it? I said to my b.w. that he would probably like to kick himself but would most likely miss.

As for Butz and his "nigger" story--he should have been fired long ago, for incompetence. A friend who found out told me just what the joke was: "All the niggers want is a tight pussy, a loose pair of shoes, and a warm place to shit". Most people feel that John W. Dean should not have publicized a private remark. My good wife and I did enjoy Butz's crack about the Pope and birth control.

I am having a colored print made from a slide portrait taken a few years ago. I have not degenerated a great deal since and I'll autograph it across the white shirt! Most people shudder when they look at my portrait, which is

112

worse than life, but you asked for it.

All the President's Men was really an unusual picture. It's the first movie I've seen, except for one or two oldies on TV, since that French one about the two girls in boarding school, and that was a good many years ago. I don't like films, but if *Roi de coeur* comes along I'll remember your recommendation.

We have had some awful weather. My b.w. has a cold- -unusual for her. I had a bad one last year, unusual for me too. I am singing Faure's *Automne*. A cold would help.

Enjoy your professional duties. Is Madame teaching or tutoring? Please give her our best wishes. Write when the spirit prompts.

Yours ever,
R. M.

Jeu d'esprit: Practical joke (witticism)
Trémas, and guillemets: Diaereses and quotation marks

Dear Mel,

Your description of Madame's cooking made my mouth water. I too married a good cook--I call her my cordon bleu. We must try to travel up to your <u>nid-d'amour</u> one of these days, responding to your most kind invitation.

I have written a little preface to the alexandrines about your trip:

A newlywed couple named Yoken
Whose French is the finest that's spoken
Set off for Paris
On a visiting spree
And brought back this verse as a token.

You are at liberty to put this into French if so minded.

The attached photo shows me in one of my grimmer moods, I'm afraid. When I get a good black and white made one of these days I'll replace it. Meantime, Cartier's has some very tasteful frames in 18k gold set with emeralds which would not be unsuitable.

Etymology has been one of my <u>violons d'Ingres</u> and so, thanks, I knew about "posh". Sometimes however, these derivations are fanciful, like the tracing of "sincere" to <u>sine cera</u>. without wax. (Pure folderol. It comes from the Latin word <u>sincerus</u>, meaning "whole.")

We sympathize with your being a victim of nepotism. The tutoring service sounds promising. All of us have had some experience of this favoritism business. Tell Miss Cindy to cheer up and remember that there's always a tomorrow. Young people are inclined to feel that opportunity knocks only once.

You are right, the typical New England accent of the kind your Boston friend demonstrates is ludicrous, as well as vulgar.

The other night I sat up for the Channel 13 presentation of *La Grande Illusion*, which after all these years and many repetitions is still, to my mind, one of the half-dozen greatest films ever made. I missed a bit of the dialogue, even with the help of English subtitles. My ear is not too sharp for French, unfortunately.

I have just learned that that scoundrel Senator Edward Gurney has been found not guilty. <u>Quo usque tandem abutere</u>... By the way, the *Times* said the other day, editorially, that Stumblebum's choice of Dole was just as bad as his pardon of Nixon. The idea of risking the future of one's country on a man not even fit to be a senator!

What do you think of Bellow as a Nobel laureate? I read one of his novels years ago, something called *Herzog*, and did not feel inclined to go on. There's too much importance attached to fiction, n'est-ce pas? I once started out to read all of Balzac. I stopped at the 40th volume out of 50. On the whole, I consider him a butcher. Is this heresy? After the four or five best, his novels seem to me contrived, fantastic, and monotonous. I still mean to re-read the *Contes Drolatiques*, however, before I'm wheeled into the <u>grand four</u> (My translation).

My old boss, a cosmopolite and a scholar, was a little coy once in a while, and once he sent the daughter of the owner of the *Sun* a present on her birthday which he described as a <u>petit cadeau</u>. I have since discovered what it means. He spoke French very well, but he didn't know that. It proves that you can't take French for granted, like the man who was frightened when he drank of a crystal lake and then saw the sign "Ce lac est bien poissonneux."

My b.w. is having a busy week--trip to the East Bronx to visit her sister tomorrow, orchestra dress rehearsal Friday night and concert Saturday night. I don't know how she stands it. They rehearse for three hours at a stretch, with perhaps a ten-minute breather. Her heart is not in the current doings--Beethoven's 7th symphony, a chestnut, and a miserable Tchaikowsky suite for a ballet company to dance. Moi, je déteste le ballet. I'd rather watch acrobats.

Little nephew (or grandson, I forget which) of our host in Uzès, a violinist named Olivier Chartier, won first at the Conservatoire last summer and seems to be headed for the big time. Watch out for him.

This is my own: do you know what's happened to the Little Moron? (figure of a series of jokes a few years ago). He has gone to Warsaw to head the University. I beg pardon of my Polish ancestors.

Yours ever,
Robert

Cordon bleu: A first-rate cook

Nid d'amour: Love nest

Violons d'Ingres: Hobbies

Quousque tandem abutere: Until when will you abuse my patience (from Cicero in his oration against Catilina)

Petit cadeau: Little gift

Ce lac est bien poissonneux: This lake is full of fish.

Moi, je déteste le ballet: As for me, I hate the ballet.

Paramus, N.J.
November 11, 1976

Dear Mel,

I am happy to know that you liked the photo. The usual publicity mug shots never really looked like me.

I am also glad you liked the limerick. I used to write a lot of them--unprintable, chiefly, for as you know

The limerick makes laughs anatomical
In a way that is most economical--
   But the good ones I've seen
   So seldom are clean,
And the clean ones so seldom are comical.

Let me also rejoice (in a good Christian spirit!) that the voting didn't go your way. I voted against continuance of the Nixon gang (most of them are still in the administration); to protect the Supreme Court against another fifth-rate tory appointee; against the Nixon pardon, which I consider little less than a crime itself--and perhaps most of all, to make it impossible for a heel like Dole to be in line for the presidency. This said, I fall back on the familiar post-election doggerel.

The election is over,
Let bitterness pass;
I'll kiss your elephant
and you.......

I'll try more Bellow on your recommendation. As for Balzac, the three novels you mention are far and away his best. I'd add *Cousin Pons* to the list.

Your test is too much for me. I still don't identify Henri Clouard or place the quotation. Or Turoldus.

The little moron joke was a feeble addition of my own to the list of Polish gags. I trust the Sherfisees (Englished spelling of my Polish forbears) are not turning over in their graves. Once one of the family in Charleston went aboard a Polish vessel and when the crew heard his name they fell to their knees. My wife, always ready with a snappy crack, said that they were lace curtain Poles. I suppose their Polish name was Czerfisi or something like that.

We have had the flu shots. No side effects.

More later.

Yours,
Robert

Paramus, N.J.
December 10, 1976

Dear Mel,

I did not mean to give the impression that I had written that limerick about limericks. It is anonymous.

I just don't get to the movies. Last I saw was *La Grande Illusion* on TV, a few days before poor Gabin died. A movie about the McCarthy witch-hunts ought to be good one.

My own golden days as a film fan date to about 1914, when I saw that wicked piece of racial propaganda, *The Birth of a Nation*. From then until we left for Philadelphia in 1918 I spent at least one afternoon a week at one of the King Street theatres in Charleston. I saw Pearl White in *The Perils of Pauline*, another serial featuring her called *The Iron Claw*, and endless Sennett, Triangle Kaybee and Charlie Chaplin two-reelers. Those old Keystone Kop movies were wonderful. Ben Turpin came along once in a while, too. And there were William S. Hart, Sessue Hayakawa, Blanche Sweet, Norma Talmadge, Pauline Frederick, and Theda Bara. A friend in Philadelphia whispered to me in an awed tone, anent her role of Cleopatra, "All she has on is a towel." She was one of the first Vamps--a rather homely little Jewish girl from Brooklyn with a pretty figure. I must not forget Fanny Ward. In New York in 1921 I saw *The Kid* for fifteen cents. Eheu fugaces. I was a Raimu-Gabin-Renoir-Fernandel fan, 1951 and earlier. But I tired of the stage and screen rather early in life. You are right, there is almost nothing "innocent" for small and larger children. For a while I loved vaudeville.

119

Thanks for clearing up the identity of Turoldus. I know only snippets from the *Chanson de Roland*. I'm also fond of *Le Cor*!

I knew, as I recall, nobody who was blacklisted by the Un-American Committee, as we used to call it. In the early 50s I was grubbing for a living as a free lance, and I knew a good many editors and a fair number of other writers. I taught several semesters as a stand-in at the Columbia School of General Studies but none of my colleagues were blacklisted as far as I know. It was a dirty business, the kind of thing Nixon was apparently aiming at. Worst thing about it was the disgusting cowardice of Eisenhower, who would not defend Gen. Marshall or even say a good word for him.

I'm sure I've read it but I have no memory of Balzac's *Le Curé de Village. Peau de Chagrin* was not one of my favorites. But as your good old Montaigne might say, Que sais-je? It may be one of the best.

I've been rather depressed by something unusual for me--a cold. It got down into my lungs and I had a nagging cough. That has cleared up now.

I do not seem to be developing a snout after having the swine flu shot. You remind me that anti-vaccination cartoons of the 18th century showed people turning into cows.

What do you think of the operatic French of so many non-French singers? Some, like Pinza, were ludicrous in their attempts to sing French--but I mean just the run-of-the-mine non-French artist. I have always hesitated to sing in French. Once I played a song recorded by Heddle Nash, good British singer, and an old French lady we are friends of said to "What language is he singing?" Not only the pronunciation but the style and voice placement are different, especially as French is a difficult language for composers to set to music because of the lack of prolonged open vowels, n'est-pas? But a good French baritone is a treat to the ear.

There is a good collection know as *The Lure of the Limerick*. Unless Miss Cindy has a fair share of the esprit Gaulois she may be shocked.

Our best wishes for the season go with this. Have a good relaxing vacation, and thank whatever gods there be that you are in your 30s. You would be astonished to know how time glides by when you are 60 or more. One New Year's Day after another. We speak of things that happened "recently" and the recently turns out to be about five years ago. Enough philosophie à dix sous!

> Yours ever,
> Robert

P.S. Are you a listener to Washington Week in Review? Peter Lisagor, one of the team and a wonderful reporter and analyst, died today. I shall miss him Friday nights.

Que sais-je: What do I know?

Esprit gaulois: Light, French humor (Gaule is the old term for France).

Philosophie à dix sous: Cheap philosophy

Paramus, N.J.
December 20, 1976

Dear Mel,

Thanks for your warm expressions of affection. I value
your friendship equally and get a lot of pleasure out of
hearing from you and writing to you. You are right about
friends--most of those I had in my youth and early maturity
are dead or far away. Hearing *Oft in the Stilly Night* is all I
need to make me break into sobs.

Christmas has become a bit too much since my
childhood. Even then people were beginning to protest the
commercialism connected with it. When my wife and I
were young she had a big family (and so did I) and we had
big Christmas parties, lots of good food and drink, laughter
and shared feelings of benevolence. When I was a child our
Christmas and New Year's tables were a refuge for all sorts
of lonely people my father dragged in--one meal I
remember was eaten by twenty-two people. We had
fireworks, a nice tree, and lots of presents, although a lot of
them cost only a few cents compared to today's greedy
prices. We tried to give my children a good time. Now they
are 38 and 35 and the younger is far off--in Houston. My
sister is 80, my older brother nearly 78 and the baby of the
family was 68 in November. I do not mean this to sound
melancholy but just to remind you that the days of our
youth are the days of our glory, as Byron said. I think the
season makes people kinder and more considerate, at least
for a little while, and the world can use a little
consideration and kindness.

My feelings about the hereafter are simple--I do not
believe in a future existence. But this calls for some

explanation.

First of all, I find it difficult to believe that any deity or other personality capable of having set in motion the endless space of which we are a microscopic part can have such a great interest in our little grain of sand. Remember, the nearest star is trillions of miles away (26 trillions!)

Why should we have been singled out for special consideration? And why are there so many cruel and useless species on our planet? Just to read about the life of insects, for example, is enough to make one agree with the liberal Protestant theologians who concede that if God is benevolent, then he cannot, in view of the enormous and sickening cruelties of the world, be omnipotent. And if he is omnipotent, he cannot be benevolent. Could he have allowed the murder of six million Jewish people by Hitler? The horrors of the Crusades and the Inquisition? The fact that half the children in the world today are starving?

Where will "souls" go? There has never been any trustworthy evidence of their survival. Fundamentally, Judaism did not believe in a future life but in fulfillment and the execution of duties in this life. I applaud that.

On the whole, I not only think reincarnation is a myth but am glad that I think so. I have enjoyed my life but once is enough. I know it is hard to feel that we are forever separated from those we have loved and cherished, and perhaps those who believe in preservation of the self or the ego are fortunate.

I consider the Christian myth only slightly superior to the myths of the Greeks, for instance. The Immaculate Conception and the Virgin birth are not terribly different from the stories of Athene's birth from the brain of Jupiter or the birth of Helen after Jupiter disguised as a swan had intercourse with Leda. I see no reason why God should have chosen a humiliating lowly origin for his son or condemned him to be scapegoat for the "sins" of the rest of mankind--such sins being, apparently, the enjoyment of the sexual process God himself devised. Why should God have kept everyone waiting until the fifth century to find that Mary was the Mother of God? And how come Jesus was born in 4 A.D., the biggest miracle of all? I think our children, and perhaps the trifles we create and the memories we leave, are a sort of immortality.

Of course you remember that Huxley refused to call himself an atheist and preferred the term agnostic--because as he said, there is no scientific proof that God does not exist. I respect the ten commandments and the sermon on the mount but I deny the divinity of Jesus, the probability of his resurrection, and still more the bodily assumption of the Blessed Virgin into heaven. Where is that? A Catholic friend of mine answers that with God all things are possible.

It is an odd thing that a lot of religious people are a great deal more afraid of death that we doubters are. I am prepared to pass on as seems to have been laid out in the scheme of things entire. I cannot shatter it to bits.

Everybody has to settle these matters for himself. I should hate to influence anyone to abandon hope, no matter how I myself feel. In the end, I comfort myself with what Heine said: "Dieu me pardonnera--c'est son métier".

It is sickening that athletics pay such disproportionate rewards. I did not know that what I call "avoir du poids" scholarships were exceeding the stipends of college professors. But the *Times* gives more space to sports, daily, than to anything else.

I have not eaten lox in recent years because the price of salmon is sky-high. We cannot even afford shrimp, really. In my childhood they were ten cents a pie plate, fresh from the fisherman's wheelbarrow. Can you imagine that?

No pun intended--but carpe diem, quam minimum credula postero.

Je vous souhaite la bonne année.

Bien à vous.
Robert

Your exams are stimulating but I must audit the course!

P.S. My better half read this letter. She adds that the business of Leda and the swan is suspiciously like the image of the holy spirit brooding over the virgin Mary in the form of a dove, after which she conceived.

You may also be interested, if you can get a copy of the January *Readers Digest*, in an article by a psychiatrist concerning the experiences related to him by people who were clinically dead and were resuscitated.

Likewise there is a chart of star distances that will appall you if you are at all like me in your reactions to immensity.

There is no reasons to allow the body to decay, a repugnant idea. I shall be cremated.

Religious has produced marvelous art and poetry and a lot of it still thrills me. Paradox? The Dies Irae still makes me shiver!

Dieu me pardonnera, c'est son métier: God will forgive me, it's his job.

Avoir du poids: To be someone of importance

Carpe diem, quam minimum credula postero: Enjoy the day, because the future should not be trusted.

Je vous souhaite la bonne année: I wish you a good new year.

Bien à vous: Truly yours

Machine à écrire: Typewriter

Dies Irae: Day of wrath. The first words of a medieval Latin hymn on the Day of Judgment sung in requiem masses.

Paramus, N.J.
January 25, 1977

Dear Mel,

It was nice of you to remember my birthday, which I shared with Richard Nixon and one or two other people. I am certainly getting into the sere and yellow. I still have thirty teeth, fair eyesight, a reasonable appetite and a good digestion. Not much energy to spare, though.

Your drama curriculum sounds very interesting. I have the (same anthology) Rhodes, but have never become familiar with any of the plays in it. Laziness. Of course I know *Pelléas and Mélisande,* as it is my favorite opera. I suppose you know that Debussy used the text of the play, with cuts? Maeterlinck wanted his wife, Georgette Leblanc, to have the title role and when it went to Mary Garden he was furious. Some say he promoted the opposition to it. I wonder that you have omitted *Pelléas*--a masterpiece of its type.

Do you know another modern play, by Tristan Bernard, which consisted of two speeches? The scene was a mountain cabin, to which a tattered fugitive came seeking refuge. He knocked and the peasant opened the door.This is the dialogue as I remember it:

Fugitive: Save me, monsieur! there is a price on my head.
Peasant: how much?
(Curtain)

The French had it in for Bernard.
Your brother's success was very good to read about.

127

I'm glad he stuck to it until he got results and I wish him fame and shekels.

Did you know that Heinrich Heine's will left everything to his wife (or mistress?) on condition that she should marry after his death? When he was asked why, he said, "Because then there will be at least one human being who will regret my passing." He is my favorite German poet. I often quote his remark: "Dieu me pardonnera. C'est son métier."

I understand your yearning to believe in a future life and of course you have a lot of company who do! The absurdities of "revealed" religion, like for instance infallibility of the Pope--and the ridiculous ignorant gaffes of the Church during the centuries, have nothing to do with one's fundamental faith. Everyone has to decide these things for himself. I recall Ford Madox Ford's story about his confession to a veteran Passionist priest in France. He said, "Father, I want to be a good Catholic, but I can't believe in the Virgin Birth and the Immaculate Conception". The oldest priest said, "My son, these are matters for theologians. You be a good boy and believe all you can."

Your translation course should be very interesting. I had a neurotic friend, a Francophile, who used to call me up about the exact meanings of phrases in French novels. It was impossible to make him understand, because of his insecurity complex, that it was impossible to render a lot of things word for word. Gide's translation of Hamlet, to judge from the soliloquy, is awful. I once read some of *Pickwick* in French. All I remember now is Mr. Winkle's description of the gun: "Il veut partir," a poor rendering of "It will go off." Did I ever tell you that the sweet old lady who translated *Pride's Way* rendered "It makes me good and tired" as "Cela me fait bon et fatigué"? She did some very clever things, otherwise. But remember the Italian motto: Traduttore, traditore.

Returning to the plays in your second set, I saw Giraudoux's *La Guerre de Troie n'aura pas lieu* on TV some years ago.

Theoretically I never make resolutions but I promise myself to do better fairly often--and don't do better. When I was first married, I gained weight so fast I had to give at least one suit away. Forty pounds in a year. Try cottage cheese, a half pound three times a day with clear tea, fresh fruit, and an occasional cracker. I took off 30 pounds that way. It was a good many years ago. I weigh 185 wearing a broad smile--sometimes 188--and should weigh about 175-180. Cottage cheese is very high in protein and you would need only vitamin pills to be on the safe side. I don't doubt that Miss Cindy is a good cook. That makes it difficult to be thin.

Our weather here has been awful. It snowed first on December 26 there is still snow on the ground looking as if it had never been touched. Last night we had another inch or two. It has been cold and windy, too. Very depressing.

My son will be thirty-nine on February 13. Try that on for feeling old!

In which cheerful vein I shall terminate this bavardage. One more thing: Try to get your translation class to give good renderings of La Rochefoucauld. That's the acid test, I think.

Yours ever,
Robert

P.S. I had more or less expected that you would be in New York for the MLA convention. Much hot air was doubtless expended.

Il veut partir: He wants to leave.

It makes me good and tired/cela me fait bon et fatigué: Cela m'épuise [in French]

Bavardage: Gossip

MLA: Modern Language Association

Letter of Louise Lévêque,
(followed by translation)

To **Robert Molloy**
Louise Lévêque
Reluires
3, villa Mozart
Paris - XVIe

Paris, le 22 juillet 1948

Cher Monsieur,

Je viens de recevoir par l'intermédiaire de la Maison Plon la lettre si touchante que vous aviez adressée à votre traducteur Jean Talva. Ce nom était le pseudonyme en littérature de ma mère, Madame Lévêque... Elle est morte, il y a presque un an (25 juillet 47...)

La traduction de *Pride's Way* est l'avant-dernière qu'elle ait faite, et je ne puis vous dire avec quelle joie, quel amusement! Votre livre lui avait profondément plu, par sa qualité d'humour, par la finesse du détail juste et vrai. Et elle avait fait tout le possible pour rendre en un français à la fois très vivant et très pur les qualités qui lui étaient si bien apparues dans le texte anglais.

J'ai la conviction personnelle que pour avoir écrit à ce sujet ce que vous avez bien voulu lui dire, il faut que vous connaissiez vous-même très bien le français. Aussi est-ce en cette langue, plus maniable pour moi, que je veux vous écrire pour vous remercier. Vous apprendrez peut-être avec étonnement que ma mère avait soixante-quinze ans quand elle a entrepris de vous traduire, et je l'entends encore rire des vieilles dames de Charleston en disant qu'il était inespéré pour elles et pour leurs idées, d'avoir trouvé une si vieille traductrice!

Ma mère était attachée à la Maison Plon et à la Maison Stock comme traductrice, depuis vingt ans, depuis la mort

132

de mon père, qui était médecin.

J'ai compté à la mort de ma chère maman près de vingt-cinq traductions. Elle a eu les deux grands prix donnés en France à ces travaux, l'un de l'Académie Française, l'autre, de fondation particulière, le prix Halpérine (qui avait été le traducteur en France des Grands Russes: Tolstoï, etc...)

D'une nature sensible et profonde, très ironique, et extrêmement cultivée, ma mère adorait l'humour. Nous vivions ensemble, à l'adresse que je vous donne ici. Sa santé ébranlée dès 45, s'est tout à fait altérée au printemps 47. Quelques jours avant sa mort, surmontant fatigue et souffrances, elle voulait encore travailler, et son dernier livre est celui d'un volume de Rosamond Lehmann dont elle a toujours été la traductrice, et qui va paraître.

J'aime personnellement beaucoup les *Voies de l'Orgueil*, il m'est aussi familier en anglais qu'en français. Je suis persuadée que si ma mère avait vécu, elle aurait toujours demandé à vous traduire et je vois par votre belle lettre que vous l'auriez aussi désiré. Je suis contente de penser que vos noms auront été associés pour le premier succès en France. Je vous en souhaite beaucoup d'autres, je suivrai votre oeuvre. Peut-être qu'un jour si vous venez à Paris, vous me ferez l'amitié de passer chez moi. Veuillez en attendant, cher Monsieur, trouver ici, mon remerciement ému et mes voeux pour votre carrière d'écrivain.

Louise Lévêque

To **Robert Molloy**
Louise Lévêque
Reluires
3, villa Mozart
Paris - XVIe   Paris, July 22th, 1948

Dear Sir,

I just received via Plon Publishers house the very touching letter that you sent to your translator Jean Talva. This name was the pseudonym used in literature by my mother, Mrs Lévêque, who died almost one year ago, 25 July 1947.

The translation of *Pride's Way* is the next to the last that she did, and I can't tell you with how much joy and pleasure. Your book deeply pleased her by its quality and its humor, by the subtlety of intricate detail. And she did her best to render in both a very lively and very pure French the qualities which were so obvious to her in the English text.

I have the personal belief that, to have written her in such a way about this matter, you must know the French language very well. So it is in this [French] language, easier for me to handle, that I want to write and thank you.

You will learn perhaps with surprise that my mother was 75 years old when she started translating your work. I hear her still laugh at the old women of Charleston saying that it was unexpected for them and for their ideas to have found such an old translator.

My mother had been working with the publishers Plon and Stock as a translator for 20 years, since the death of my father, who was a doctor.

134

I counted at the death of my dear mother, nearly 25 translations. She received the greatest prizes which are given in France to this type of work, one from the French Academy and the other from a private foundation, the Halperine Prize (Halperine was the translator in France of the great Russians: Tolstoï, etc...)

My mother had a deep and sensitive character, very ironic, and extremely cultured, she loved humor. We lived together, at the address that I give you here. Her health, poor ever since 1945, deteriorated badly in the spring of 1947. Some days before her death, overcoming fatigue and suffering, she still wanted to work, and her last work is a volume by Rosemond Lehmann whose translator she has always been. This volume will be published soon.

I personally love *Pride's Way*. It is equally familiar for me both in French and English. I am convinced that if my mother had lived longer, she would have always wanted to translate your work, and I see in your beautiful letter that you would have liked it, too. I am happy thinking that your names have been associated for this first success in France. I wish you many others, and I will follow your work. Maybe, one day, if you come to Paris, you will give me the pleasure of visiting me. While awaiting that time, dear sir, please accept my sincere thanks and by best wishes for your literary career.

Louise Lévêque

Memoir of Robert Molloy
by Marion Molloy

Robert Molloy: A Memoir

When I was asked to write this little memoir of my husband, I sat down and tried to decide what he was really like, what were his characteristics and attitudes. I knew him intimately for fifty years, and can list many facets of his personality, that I knew so well. He was intellectually brilliant, quick to grasp whatever interested him and as quick to discard what he found no use for. He was a member of the Mensa Society, but he did not attend many meetings. There was too much emphasis on popular diversions, like bridge playing of jazz which had no appeal for him.

He was a very social and gregarious person but only with people he liked and felt at home with. He hated cocktail parties and literary teas, and preferred small groups, family members or close friends...

He had a keen sense of humor and the ridiculous, as his readers know. He loved jokes and anecdotes. All the Molloy brothers were wonderful story tellers, who loved to recall their boyhood doings and the amusing people and incidents they recalled. Looking back on our young years together, it seems to me we were always laughing.

But none of this tells you what he was really like, and thinking about him I have decided that what I chiefly remember is his zest for life. He had many passionate interests and what he loved he continued to love as long as he lived. No stretch of time was long enough for all he wanted to know and to do. He added to his knowledge steadily for more than seventy years, and was still studying and reading the week he died. His interests were all in the humanities. He had no scientific bent or mathematical leanings. He read enough in such fields to be literate in them, but his real passions were for literature, history, philosophy, music, languages.

Anyone who has read his books knows that my husband's strongest memories were of his boyhood years and the place of his birth. All his books are about South Carolina; even the later novels, set in and around New York, are still really about Charleston. The characters all have their roots there, and are about old friends and relatives remembered from younger days. This seems surprising when you realize how short a time he lived in the south and in what different scenes all the rest of his life was passed.

Robert Molloy was born in Charleston, South Carolina, in 1906, the next to the youngest of a family of five. They were comfortably off and middle class, established there for several generations and well-respected by neighbors and fellow townsmen. But when Robert was in his early teens, his father had business reverses, and the family moved to the north and established themselves in New York. From then on, Robert lived a very different life, no longer prosperous nor an integral part of a homogeneous society. Except for an occasional visit, he never spent any time in Charleston again. It was a complete break with the past. And yet, in a way, he never left Charleston and never put the past behind him. He lived all the rest of his life in a state of nostalgia for Charleston. We were married for forty-eight years and, in all that time, there was rarely a day when he did not speak of those years and some memory that he recalled fondly...

It was a good time to be young and a good place to spend a childhood. Robert's family lived in a big house with many rooms and fireplaces and wood stoves. It stood in a wide lawn and garden, and had big shady piazzas upstairs and down, where the children could play. Anyone who had read *Pride's Way* knows about the family, which was pictured in the O' Donnells. Robert had two older brothers and a sister, and a younger brother, close to him in age. Also, and most important in his life, was a grandmother who lived with them. She was his mother's mother, half French, and a source of great comfort to the two smallest boys. She talked to them, sang to them, sympathized with them in times of trouble, supervised their prayers and made them laugh with her jokes and stories.

Next in importance was the nurse, Maggie, who stayed with them for years, after the family no longer needed a nursemaid. In the later years, she served as housekeeper and maid. Her husband was also a member of the family. He was a large, handsome man who had the sonorous name of Braxton Bragg, after the Civil War general, but who was always known by the childhood nickname of Bubba. Maggie and Bubba also lived in the family house, having rooms in the back, and Bubba was yardman and handyman. He was a splendid storyteller, much loved by the children. Maggie and Bubba came to New York when war industries attracted workers from the south and, years later, in New York, Maggie was nurse to my two small boys. Besides Maggie there was a cook and housemaid in the Charleston house, and once a week a laundress who carried home the great heaps of laundry which she washed and dried in her own backyard and brought back the next week.

Maggie was a small, animated woman, a wonderful mimic and a brilliant raconteuse of gossip and Charleston legends. She had had a sad life. She told me once she was married at fourteen and had <u>twelve</u> children, every one of which was born dead or died shortly after birth. Bubba was reputed to be a Lothario, and I am afraid he must have had syphilis, but, in those more innocent days, nobody apparently thought of it. However both Maggie and Bubba lived to be long past eighty. We went to Maggie's funeral, and she was buried way out in Queens somewhere, as far afield from Charleston and her youth as can be imagined.

The change from Charleston to New York must have been a wrench to the whole family. The two oldest boys were away from home and the only sister was married and living in New Jersey. The diminished family lived in a city apartment and the two youngest boys, Robert and Charles, went to big city schools, played in city parks, rode in subway cars and trolleys and never lived in Charleston again. But Robert never forgot it, and he never in fifty years lost all his Charleston accent.

Charleston speech is unique, quite different from other "southern accents." It is clipped and clear, and its vowel sounds are without the drawled diphthongs that mar so much American speech. Only the educated Irish have such pure, unmodified vowel sounds. Charleston speech often puzzles people who hear it for the first time.

Coming to New York, Robert was much stuck by the strange sounds he heard all around him. He once came home and told me how he had gone to the help of a small child who had fallen down and heard the grateful mother say to the child, "Say thenk you to the meeyun."

Charleston children also learned to speak Gullah, which is a local dialect, part English and part African, spoken by the black people along the coast. Of late years there has been a revived interest in Gullah and recently a translation of the Bible into the dialect. When Robert was a boy it was only an amusing form of speech, much enjoyed by children; however, speaking Gullah was regarded as misconduct by elders and teachers, and if you wanted to be known as a daring rebel against authority, you were heard talking Gullah with your friends. Maggie sang songs in Gullah, and Robert later sang them to his sons.

Charleston, like other Southern cities, had favorite

foods, and Robert looked back on them with pleasure. When I was married, I had to learn to prepare several of them. Hoppinjohn was one he loved, and Maggie taught me how to make it. It was really an acquired taste and it took me a while to get used to it. It was a Caribbean sort of dish, a mixture of rice and clay peas which are actually a kind of dried beans that get their name because they taste exactly like clay. It is flavored with salt pork and abundant black pepper. I suppose vegetarians would say it is a complete protein and very nutritious and inexpensive, but my boys did not like it. It wasn't easy to cook it because in our young days you couldn't buy clay peas in every grocery store. Someone had to bring it from Harlem.

Another Charleston dish was known as "gateau potate," which was a bastard French name for a sort of sweet potato soufflé. It is made of mashed sweet potatoes and beaten eggs, the whole highly flavored with cinnamon, and baked to a fluffy consistency. I liked gateau potate but haven't been able to prepare it in years, because I can no longer buy sweet potatoes--only yams which are a completely different plant.

Hominy grits I knew from my own childhood, because my father had lived in the South as a young man, and my mother used to cook it for him. In Charleston, it was served with freshly caught shrimp, brought in by the shrimp boats early in the morning. It was a breakfast dish; the shrimp had to be icy cold and the hominy fiery hot and lavishly dressed with butter. In New York, the Molloys no longer had a cook or Maggie, and Robert's mother, who had never run a house, must have been lost and unhappy.

The two youngest boys who were still at home were admitted to New York schools, the first big city schools they had ever attended. Robert was a brilliant student and much admired by his teachers, who expected great things of him. He was valedictorian of his class and made a speech at his graduation exercises that was always being cited to me, because I was valedictorian of the next class. The whole time I was preparing my speech, I was being reminded of "Molloy's speech" and urged to equal it in wit and style of delivery.

We had met for the first time that year in a Latin class. Although I was a year behind him in school, there were not many young people reading four years of Latin. Only old-fashioned parents expected such diligence from their teen-agers. Classes had to be merged, and so we were assigned to the same Latin teacher.

Robert was an excellent scholar; in fact, he laid the groundwork there for another of his life-long passions. He read Latin all his life, a portion almost every day, and built up a large library of Latin authors and poets, both classical and medieval. I am afraid I was a disappointment to him. I liked Latin and did well in school, but soon lost my enthusiasm and consequently my ability to read it easily.

The boys' father died suddenly when Robert was about to graduate, and their life changed again abruptly. They were left without money and dependent on the older boys, who were married and raising childen of their own. There was no money for college, and Robert had to set out at once and find work. For several years, he struggled along, going from one low-paid job to another. He worked as a night bank clerk for a while, and came home in the middle of the night in the subway. He would ask the subway guard to wake him when the train got to his stop, and then he would sleep soundly all the way home. Usually he was wakened in time, but occasionally he was carried all the way to Van Cortlandt Park, and then he would have to take a downtown train back again to Washington Heights. He would stand all the way back so as not to fall asleep again. He was over six feet tall, extremely thin, and his mother worried about him.

There was another job that he found and that he loved very much and kept on with for several years; he was an usher at Carnegie Hall and at the Metropolitan Opera House. That did not take his full time and left him free for other work. It did not pay very much but there were always many applicants for the work. The young people who ushered were a very friendly group, all eager to talk about their interests and their hopes. They were mostly music students, violinists, pianists, singers, young people from small towns, aspirants to the concert, opera stage and to Broadway musicals. Ushering left them time to practice and rehearse. After evening performances, they would go in a large group to a nearby cafeteria to discuss the performances they had heard.

Finally Robert found more permanent and better paying work, selling advertising for Donnelly's Red Book and he stuck there for a while. There never was anyone less suited for going about town trying to sell anything to reluctant tradesmen. He wasn't very successful at it, but one of his older brothers had a position with the firm, and he gave Robert help and encouragement. We were planning to marry, were hunting for an apartment and choosing furniture. We had a strict budget for everything and had vowed not to pay more than fifty dollars a month for our apartment, but finally gave in and paid fifty-two for a lovely three-room garden apartment. I was a beginning teacher in a New York City school, and we felt we could manage this extravagance because I was earning more than one hundred dollars a month. We had no doubts about our golden future, and so we were married on 29 June 1929, a portentous date.

By that winter we were struggling to keep our heads above water. My salary was assured because I had tenure in the school system, but Robert was out of work like everyone else around us. Again he tried all sorts of work, some that he liked and some that he hated but he made a number of acquaintances here and there. One occupation he was good at was reading manuscripts for publishers and he soon began to get books to review and so took his first steps toward a literary career. It would seem that he had had little interest in writing so far, but in reality he had written his first full-length novel by the time he was twenty. With the optimism of youth and his complete innocence of literary usage, he had sent it off to various publishers without the help of an agent. Naturally it came back to him every time and he finally gave up on it and put it away. He was rather ashamed of this youthful manuscript, and would not let me read it, so I never saw it. But I don't doubt it was still there, buried under the mountains of papers that he left to the University of South Carolina when he died.

After a year or two, he made the acquaintance of Madeleine Boyd, the widow of Ernest Boyd, the critic, and she asked him to help her translate some French stories. He also did a number of Spanish translations, and so began to make a little place for himself. He did book reviews quite regularly for the New York *Sun*, a solid, conservative, family-oriented newspaper. The literary editor of the Sun was James Grey, who liked Robert and his work, and offered him a place as his assistant in 1936. This was only a part-time job at first, and the *Sun* put him on its copy desk to fill out his week's hours. Both positions were well suited to his abilities, and he was always glad he had had the opportunity to learn copy editing. He was a meticulous editor, and a purist about the English language.

He made many warm friends at the Sun, among them William McFee, the British novelist, who took a great interest in Robert. McFee was totally deaf for most of his adult life, so the friendship was carried on by letters. They wrote to each other every few weeks for many years, until McFee died, a very old man.

After some years, Mr. Grey's health began to fail and Robert took over more and more of the literary page. When Mr. Grey died the *Sun* made Robert literary editor. He had not forgotten he wanted to write, and decided to take a course in short story writing. The instructor was Sylvia Chatfield Bates, a successful writer in the period between the two World Wars. She was a stimulating teacher, and under her influence he wrote some short stories based on his Charleston years. He sent them to various magazines and they were all published. Then Miss Bates suggested that he try a novel with the same sort of material. He promptly wrote *Pride's Way* which was accepted by Macmillan and was a Literary Guild selection for that year, 1945.

From then on, he wrote steadily for a number of years; *Uneasy Spring* in 1946, the first book with a New York background. In 1949 came *Best of Intentions* in 1950, *Pound Foolish* and, in 1953, *A Multitude of Sins*, all three laid in Charleston. In 1958, he wrote *An Afternoon in March*, which was a re-telling of a Charleston murder, notorious in its days. The last were *The Reunion* in 1959, and *The Other Side of the Hill* in 1962, both laid in the north but with strong links with Charleston.

He also wrote one non-fiction book: *Charleston: A Gracious Heritage* in 1947. It was one in the Appleton-Century American Cities series, beautifully illustrated by E.H. Suydam. This was a very successful and much admired book, a great hit in Charleston itself and well reviewed everywhere. Of course, it is by now out-of-date. The late years of the city are not there, but as far as it goes, it is even now a wonderful evocation of a unique city's personality; Charleston still loves it. The last time we visited there in 1973, we found the book for sale in Legerton's book store.

I have traced his literary life from the first unpublished work of his late teens through the entire output of his later years. But writing was only one of a number of consuming interests that filled his mind and absorbed his concentrated attention all his life. In fact, for many years, it was secondary to his most ardent love of music. From his boyhood, he was passionately interested in playing and listening to music, and he tried to persuade his father to let him learn to play the piano. Oddly enough, in that big family he was the only one in whom musical talent appeared, although it skipped a generation and showed up in some of his brother's children and grandchildren. His father by no means approved of Robert's spending time and money on such a pursuit, and only consented to the lessons on condition that he was never to practice when his father was at home. Of course, musical talent doesn't flourish with such restrictions, and he never became more than a good amateur player, though he continued to study after his father died, with not much money or time to give to it. When we met again, a few years after we left high school, he was taking lessons from Clarence Adler, a concert artist and teacher.

Robert knew he could not make a career of the piano, but he never gave it up in discouragement or disgust. He continued to play and occasionally to study all the rest of his life whenever he had time to give to it. When we were married, the first thing we bought for our new home was a Baldwin baby grand piano. We had no rug for the living room floor and no curtains for the windows, but we squeezed out the money for that piano. One of the reasons we took that expensive apartment was that it had a living room big enough to hold it.

In the several years before we were married, we lived a life completely surrounded by music. Robert, in his years of ushering, had heard all the great musicians of the 1920's. He listened over and over to Rachmaninoff, Rubinstein, Gabrilowich, Hoffman. He carried his piano music with him and pored over them while he listened. He heard the famous orchestras and the most admired conductors. He heard violinists, Fritz Kreisler, Jascha Heifetz, Mischa Elman. He heard John McCormack singing Mozart, Bach, German Lieder... He made the acquaintance of the world of opera. So the months spent at Carnegie Hall and the Metropolitan Opera gave him a wonderful musical foundation because he was so ready to receive it and he built on that foundation all his life.

We used to go to Carnegie Hall every few weeks, usually on student passes. We sat far up in the back or around on the side, nearly out of sight of the performer. I first heard John McCormack while we sat on the side steps of the top balcony. We went to hear *Pelléas et Mélisande* standing at the back of the top balcony. After that we bought the French recording and played it until we knew every word and note by heart. Both our families lived in Washington Heights and within easy walking distance of the Lewisohn Stadium, where for twenty-five cents one could sit oudoors on summer evenings and hear the New York Philharmonic and watch the moon come up.

I was a violinist, very modest in ability but able to play chamber music, and we played all the violin and piano sonatas, one after another.

Along with this absorption in music. Robert did not forget his interest in languages. As soon as he began ushering at the Metropolitan and following the libretti, he threw himself into learning the new langages. He had studied Spanish in school and at once discovered he could read Italian with no trouble. He decided to add French and German to his list, and in no time could read them. With his usual enthusiasm, he set himself to perfecting his accent in both and succeeded to a remarkable extent. He attended foreign language movies over and over to study the pronunciation... I can't recall how many times we saw *La Grande Illusion*, *La Kermesse héroïque* and *The Baker's Wife*. We went regularly to the old Thalia Theater on Broadway. (It just closed its doors in 1987, and a part of our youth is gone with it.) Robert also bought hundreds of foreign records, some by actors and some teaching records.

When he began reading manuscripts for publishers, he told them he could read several languages and began to receive French, Italian and Spanish work to evaluate. He was less sure of his German and continued to work on perfecting that. He was asked to write articles on European literature for the first edition of the Columbia Encyclopedia and, in doing research for that, he discovered he could read several other languages, notably Dutch and Rumanian, with their roots in German and Latin.

Robert translated a number of Spanish books and so filled in many empty spaces in his career when he had no new work of his own in hand. He translated *Doña Barbara* by Rómulo Gallegos in 1931, while he was still struggling with the depression, and that was the first of a number of translations from the Spanish. Over the years he did the novels of Luis Spota and the Latin American political books by Victor Alba. This was a subject on which Robert felt himself not very well informed, and which was, therefore, really hard work. But all the authors approved Robert's work, and he became known as a reliable translator.

I had been teaching for several years in the lower grades of a city elementary school, and I was preparing myself for a promotion license to teach at the intermediate level. My subject was music and, while I played the piano and the violin, I felt I ought to have some instruction in vocal technique, so I began taking voice lessons. At once, Robert was fascinated by this new suject and decided to study with the same teacher. Robert had a pleasant bass baritone voice, not at all of performance quality, but then he wasn't interested in performing. It was learning the proper method of voice production he was after, and how to present songs and arias. We studied with a Russian soprano who had been a member of the Chicago Opera Company. She had also been successful on the recital stage. She was adept at various styles of singing and was a wonderful tutor in the pronunciation of all modern European languages. Robert had a splendid time pursuing this new interest. He acquired a large repertoire of both songs and opera arias. He joined the Henry Street Music School opera class where he had the great delight of singing the part of Figaro in a production of *Le Nozze di Figaro*. Then he studied for a number of years with Frazer Gange, a British baritone who sang many recitals in this country.

We had two sons and decided to leave the city and buy a house in New Jersey. We chose a town where the schools were good and where an active music life was to be found. Both boys had very early showed signs of unusual musical ability and Robert, remembering his own childhood frustrations, gave them every encouragement. They both began to study early and heard good music and first rate performers from their cradles. They also inherited Robert's extraordinary flair for languages. As small children they would sing, as they played in their swing, Italian arias in perfect Italian, just from listening to the records, not of course understanding the words they sang. They both had absolute pitch and that keenness of ear made the language sounds clear to them. Both boys went to music schools, one to Juilliard and one to the Leopold Mannes; both are professional musicians today. This was a great source of pleasure and satisfaction to Robert. With his brothers, he could talk about Charleston but with his sons he could talk about music and that is a subject that never palls and never ends.

The New Jersey town where we first lived had a very good symphony orchestra, made up of both amateurs and professional players. One of Robert's nephews played in it and at Robert's urging I applied to join it. I didn't feel myself really qualified, but I was accepted, and played in the string section for thirty years. Robert was at once fired with the desire to learn another instrument and rashly undertook to take up the cello. This was one time he had to accept partial defeat. All the stringed instruments are difficult to play and the cello is probably the hardest. He bought a cello and arranged for lessons from a member of the orchestra but he never attained any real facility. He stuck to it for a long time, but finally decided he had no hope of achieving real ease and reluctantly gave it up. He felt it was a little too late to perfect a new technique.

But it was not too late to follow all his lifelong interests and pleasures. Robert was one man to whom retirement brought only pleasant anticipation. He had been working part time on the copy desk of the New York *Daily News*, because he felt he had a sort of block in his writing. At the same time he became interested in hypnotism. He had heard that Rachmaninoff, having lost his musical inspiration, had had himself hypnotized and thereafter wrote his greatest concerto. Robert, always interested in something new, decided to try it. He found a well-recommended practitioner, who taught him the art of self-hypnotism and, at once, he discovered he had a wonderful tool. The first and one of the best results was in the relief of pain. All his life Robert had suffered from severe attacks of migraine at regular intervals. They began with visual disturbances and flickering lights, followed by almost total blindness, then disabling pain and nausea. He was incapacited for at least twenty-four hours at a time. Medicine did not help; he just had to endure it until it was over. By chance, he discovered that by self-hypnosis he could abort the attack at the first eye symptom, and never had a severe migraine again. He applied this ability to the dentist office and found it worked as well there. He never again needed novocaine for any dental operation.

In his later years, he had open-heart surgery and eased the pain of the post-operational days with this skill. He couldn't explain how he did it. When asked how he did it, he said, "I just dismiss the pain and it goes away." He never wrote that great last novel he had aimed for, but he felt he had an even better result.

Robert and I retired after the heart operation. We travelled for a while and then he settled down to really enjoy and use his new freedom. He planned a daily routine, so many hours for writing, regular times for study and for practicing and singing. He continued perfecting his knowledge of German and French, from records and television programs, and, of course, by endless reading. He was a wonderful traveling companion anywhere in Europe, because he was never at a loss for words.

These retirement years seemed to him the right time to correct what he felt was a lapse in his education. All his life he had regretted that he did not know Greek, so he now set to work to learn it. And learn it he did! Before he died, he had read the *New Testament* in Greek, and had started on the classic writers. If he had only had five more years he would have done wonders. He continued to read Latin regularly, and hoped to be as knowledgeable in Greek.

Meantime, he wanted to keep on with his music. He found a piano teacher and a vocal coach in our New Jersey community of Paramus, and began to add to his repertoire in both arts. He took along a cassette to each lesson, recorded his performance and his teachers' comments and played them over when he practiced.

He planned to leave all his literary remains to the University of South Carolina, not because he had ever been there, but because the University asked him to let them have the papers for their special library of South Carolina authors. He left an enormous mass of papers, all his munuscripts, published and unpublished, copies of all his books, in English and in translation, magazines with his short stories in them, contracts and letters from his various agents and publishers, correspondence with many friends and acquaintances, scrapbooks of all the reviews he had written in his younger years, and reviews of all his own work. I am not sure what else was left, as the University asked me not to sort it out, but to leave that to them. I forget how many large cartons I packed and sent off to Columbia, S.C., but I think there were at least seven. I don't think that Robert had actually looked at that heap of papers in a long time, but he probably thought some day he would get around to sorting it.

Meantime he was too busy. In the week he died, he had a piano lesson and a vocal tutoring. He was active and happy to the end. On the morning after the voice lesson, he got up, ate breakfast and was sitting in the living room, reading the New York *Times*, when he suddenly closed his eyes and, in a moment, was gone. It was a peaceful ending to a full and happy life.

Marion Molloy
October 1987

Index

Dr. Minxit (character in Claude Tillier's novel, <u>Mon Oncle Benjamin</u>); 92
Dr. *Zhivago* (Boris Pasternak); 57
D*uchess of Malfi, The* (John Webster); 56
Du Maurier, George; 94
Duparc, Henri; 78

Education of Henry Adams, The (Henry Adams); 94
Edward the Second (Christopher Marlowe); 56
Eiseley, Loren; 101
Eisenhower, Dwight; 32, 106, 120
El Verdugo (cf. Franco); 62, 65
Elman, Mischa; 147
Emerson, Ralph Waldo; 20, 90
Enfants du paradis, Les (Marcel. Carné, dir.); 74, 81
Espy, Willard R.; 94

Faulkner, William; 105
Fauré, Gabriel; 51, 70, 113
F*emme du Boulanger, La* (Marcel Pagnol, dir.,
        <u>The Baker's Wife</u>, eng); 74, 148
Ferdinand the Bull (Munro Leaf); 23, 24
Ferguson, Marilyn; 44
Fernandel; 119
Flaubert, Gustave; 23, 75, 77
F*ood of the Gods, The* (H.G. Wells); 107
Ford, Ford Madox; 52, 128
Ford, Gerald; 60, 100, 106, 109
France, Anatole; 14, 18, 82
Franco, Francisco [cf. El Verdugo]; 68
Frederick of Prussia; 39
Frederick, Pauline; 119
Fremont-Smith, Eliot; 64
F*rench in the Air*; 18, 60
Frost, Robert; 90

Gabin, Jean; 119
Gabrilowitsch, Ossip; 147
Gallegos, Rómulo; 148

Osservatore; 50
Our Crowd (Stephen Birmingham); 89
Owl and the Pussycat, The; 81
Oxford Companion, The; 57, 62

Palès (cf André Chénier); 96, 97
Pangloss; 73
Peanuts (Charles Schultz); 30, 55
Peau de Chagrin, La (Honoré de Balzac); 120
Pelléas and Mélisande (Maurice Maeterlinck); 127, 147
PEN; 78
Pepys, Samuel; 22
Père Goriot, Le (Honoré de Balzac); 8
Perils of Pauline, The (movie); 119
Pickwick (Charles Dickens); 128
Pinza, Ezio; 120
Portnoy's Complaint (Philip Roth); 25, 58, 105
Practical Cogitator, The (Curtis and Greenslet); 57
Prisoner of Zenda, The (movie); 105
Proust, Marcel; 81, 85

Rabelais; 70
Rachnaninoff, Sergheï; 147, 150
Racine, Jean; 51
Radio Diffusion Française; 60
Raimu; 119
Reader's Digest, The; 51, 125
Reagan, Ronald; 105, 106
Renard, Jules; 41
Renoir, Jean; 119
Reynolds, Paul; 92
Robespierre; 96
Roi de Coeur (movie); 113
Romains, Jules; 57
Roosevelt, Franklin D.; 109
Roosevelt, Theodore; 97
Rouge et le Noir, Le (Stendhal); 24
Rubinstein, Arthur; 114

Rusher William A.; 102
Ruskin, John; 56

Saison en Enfer, Une (Arthur Rimbaud); 72
Sanctuary (William Faulkner); 105
Sand, George; 68, 72, 74, 75, 77, 94
Sarraute, Nathalie; 35
Scheier, Morris; 94
Schopenhauer, Arthur; 25
Schumann, Robert; 22
Schwartz, Delmore; 72
Schweicker, Richard; 105, 106
Scott, Sir Walter; 18, 23, 41, 110
Seconde, La (Colette); 72
Selassie, Haile; 50
Sennett, Mark; 119
Sevareid, Eric; 104
Sévigné, Mme de; 12
Shannon, William V.; 109
Show Me (book); 61, 64
Simpson, Louis; 72
Since Yesterday (Frederick Lewis Allen); 108
SMU (Southeastern Massachusetts University); 24
Socrates; 106
Spota, Luis; 148
Steegmuller, Francis; 81
Steinbeck, John; 105
Stevenson, Robert Louis; 98
Stirling, Jane; 77
Strachey, Lytton; 83
Stravinsky, Igor; 35
Suydam, E.H.; 27, 145
Sweet, Blanche; 119

Tales of Genji, The (book); 103
Talmadge, Norma; 119
Talva, Jean; 5, 132, 134
Tartarin de Tarascon (Alphonse Daudet); 8
Tchaikovsky, Peter; 116

Thackeray, William; 89
Thaïs, (Anatole France); 47, 82
The Sound and the Fury (William Faulkner); 105
This Was Cicero (H.J. Haskell); 51
Tillier, Claude; 5, 18, 87, 91, 92, 95
Tolstoï, Count Lev; 133, 135
Trollope, Anthony; 57
Truman, Harry; 32, 84
Turoldus; 118, 120
Turpin, Ben; 119
Twain, Mark; 67
Twayne, Publishing Company; 5, 18, 91, 97
Typee (Herman Melville); 98

Vanity Fair (William, Thackeray); 89
Vaugelas; 98
Verdurins, les; 82, 85
Verne, Jules; 81, 92
Villon, François; 52, 62
Vingt mille lieues sous les Mers (Jules Verne); 81
Voltaire; 39

Wallace, Georges; 79, 84
Ward, Fanny; 119
Washington Week in Review; 56, 121
Washington, George; 71
Watergate; 116
Weight Watchers Magazine; 80, 83
Wells, H. G.; 107
White, Pearl; 119
Whitman, Walt; 90
Wilson, Sloan; 40
WNCN (Radio station); 47
WNET (Television station); 32
WNYC (Radio station); 60, 74
Wodehouse, P.G.; 23, 55, 62, 96
Words at Play (Willard R. Espy), 94

STUDIES IN AMERICAN LITERATURE